# Contents

# Preface

The period covered by this book is described rather loosely as 'the early years', which in practice means canals begun before 1790. The date is not arbitrary. After an initial burst of enthusiasm following the widely publicized success of the Duke of Bridgewater's Canal, everything ground to a halt. It was not the result of a sudden lack of interest in canals, but reflected a paralysing slump in the national economy caused by the American War of Independence. Even when matters were resolved by the Peace of Versailles in 1783, the economy recovered sluggishly. When canal building began again with renewed enthusiasm, the first generation of engineers had either died or retired and the work passed to new men with new ideas. The result was that the post-1790 canals generally have very different characteristics from their predecessors, using different engineering techniques and different materials, notably cast iron.

One problem that had to be faced when dealing with the early years was what to do about canals that had changed considerably during their working days. In the case of canals where the construction period extended well beyond 1790 – the Leeds & Liverpool is the outstanding example – the canals have simply been covered from beginning to end, regardless of when a particular section was built during the long process of construction. A quite different problem is posed by canals that were completed and then subsequently altered to a great extent, as happened on the Birmingham Canal and the northern end of the Oxford. Here, I have only dealt with the canals as originally built, as the alterations involved work characteristic of a much later age.

The aim has been to provide a full survey of the canals of the period. One rather obvious omission is the little privately-developed Ketley Canal, with its inclined plane built by William Reynolds. There are two reasons for its omission. The first is that there is very little left to see, and the second is that it seemed more appropriate to hold back a discussion of the inclined planes to the period to be covered in the next volume, when they played a more important role in canal building. Wales is not covered for the very good reason that no Welsh canals were built during this period. Although there was one important Scottish canal, the Forth and Clyde, it too has been omitted, but will put in an appearance later, when it can be put in context with the other Scottish canals.

In writing this book, I have tried to keep up with the constantly changing world of the canals. The greatest changes are found in the world of restoration. My last visit to a canal site was made literally a couple of weeks before completing the manuscript. I went to renew my acquaintance with the

Chesterfield Canal, and found a lot of work in progress: by the time this book is read, some sections of canals that were then derelict will be open. I have not attempted to guess what the new will be like. Similarly, Derek Pratt is constantly travelling the whole system, ensuring his photographs are right up to date. It has been very interesting comparing the pictures in the books on which we have collaborated with those of today. In some places little has changed, in others the scenes are scarcely recognizable. Things never stand still; waterways, which are now part of the leisure industry, are not going to look as they did when they were the main arteries of commerce. What we have tried to do, in words and pictures, is to convey as much as possible of the original character of each waterway, and show how it developed as a response to the landscape through which it was built and as the result of a series of decisions taken by individual engineers and builders.

Anthony Burton
Stroud, 2001

# 1. Beginnings

It is commonplace to describe the Canal Age as beginning in 1760 with the construction of the Bridgewater Canal from the coal mines of Worsley to Manchester. In the sense that this canal was the first wholly artificial waterway in Britain, with a course unrelated to any natural river or stream, this is true, though even then one has to ignore the existence of Ireland. But the Bridgewater Canal did not appear from nowhere, in a sort of navigational equivalent of the Big Bang. It would be more accurate to describe it as representing an important stage in the long history of inland waterways. This book will be looking specifically at artificial canals, but it is impossible to make sense of their development and structures without an understanding of what went before, and not just in Britain. There has been a tendency among authors, and present company is most certainly not excepted, to treat the history of Britain's canals as though it existed in isolation. It is a very misleading view to adopt. This first chapter, therefore, will be a brief gallop across the centuries that led up to the events of 1760.

No one can say with any certainty when rivers were first used for transport, other than that it happened at some time in prehistory, before the appearance of written records. Speculation that the blue stones from the Preseli Hills in Wales made at least part of their journey to Stonehenge by being rafted down the Hampshire Avon remain just that – speculation. What we can say with certainty is that substantial boats were being built and used on the Humber back in the Bronze Age, for their remains were discovered in the mud at North Ferriby and dated around BC1500. Hundreds of miles of river were navigable in Britain without man making any effort to alter their natural course and flow, so their history does not really form a part of this particular story. Just when did man begin to tamper with rivers to make for easier navigation or to open up new areas for water transport? No definite dates can be set, but at least we can say with confidence that real changes began with the arrival of the Romans.

It is well known that Roman engineers built lengthy canals, complete with imposing aqueducts, but these were mainly used for water supply. More importantly for British waterways history, they also built canals to drain marshland, and there are notable examples in the Fens of England. The best known of these is the Car Dyke, which was built from the River Cam to the Great Ouse. It is a substantial work with sloping sides, a flat bottom, and is approximately six feet deep. Earlier archaeological reference books speak of it as being built partly for drainage, but also as intended for navigation, to carry grain to Roman garrisons. Newer works now discount the navigational aspects, but that does not mean that once the canal was completed it was not used by boats, simply that the use is not recorded. Even if not built with boats in mind, it would be odd if such a convenient waterway was not used occasionally, just as Fen drainage ditches of later years were to be used. One aspect of Roman construction was to reach down through the centuries – the use of puddled clay to make watertight linings. Puddle generally consists of a sloppy mixture of clay and water, stiffened with sand or gravel, that could then be pressed into place to make a lining, and not just for canals. We know, for example, that large quantities of puddle were used in the building of Hadrian's Wall.

The Romans also introduced a device into Britain which might not seem to have a great deal to do with navigation – the waterwheel of the type first devised by Vitruvius in the 1st century BC. This is the familiar vertical wheel that we see in the great majority of water mills that have survived in Britain. It took over from the horizontal wheel which, like a turbine, was set directly into a fast flowing river or stream to turn a vertical shaft which then drove the millstones directly. The new Roman mills had to have gearing to convert the rotation of the horizontal shaft to the vertical shaft holding the stones, and that meant that they needed some means of ensuring a regular motion. The simplest method was to dam up the stream to create a millpond and then regulate the flow of water through sluices. Today the watermill tends to be viewed as a rather quaint, picturesque survivor, but there was a time when it was a vital part of the life of the whole country. Jumping ahead through the centuries, to the time when William I ordered that great survey of his new kingdom, the Domesday Book, it was recorded that there were an astonishing 5,624 watermills south of the Trent.

The implications of this for other river users were immense. The millers soon discovered that an efficient way of ensuring a good water supply was to build a weir across the river, so that water could be channelled down a leat to the wheel. A huge dam right across a river might seem an impassable barrier to boats, but it turned out to be a blessing. The problem with all rivers is that they infuriatingly refuse to flow in a neat, orderly manner: sometimes deep, sometimes shallow, in some places dawdling and lethargic, in others dashing and energetic. Above a weir, the water is deepened and tamed to placidity. This makes it a great deal more convenient for boating. Now all that was needed was some means of getting the boat across the dam. The answer was a device variously known as stanch, staunch or flash lock.

The earliest recorded reference to a flash lock in Britain is to one on the Thames at Marlow in 1306. It was to develop into quite a sophisticated device. The easiest way to think of it is as a gate let into the weir. It consisted of a stout wooden beam at the bottom, with an upper beam extended as a balance beam for easy opening. The space in between consisted of fixed vertical bars, known as 'rimers' and between these there were removable wooden slats, known as 'paddles' or 'lock gates', because they locked the gate together. When a boat wanted to pass, the paddles were removed – the gate was unlocked – allowing the water to flow. When the flow had moderated, the main frame could be swung aside by the balance beam. Boats heading downstream could ride the "flash" of water through the weir, while those heading in the opposite direction were generally winched up by means of a capstan. Not only did the flash lock get the boats across the weir, it brought other advantages as well. It helped boats heading downstream to ease their way across the shallows, carried along on the flood of water. Upstream of the weir, the increased depth of water soon built up again to allow boats to proceed on their way on calm waters. There was also, however, a big disadvantage for the boats heading down through the lock. It required a nice judgement to time the descent. Set off too soon and there was a real danger of a capsize in the violent flow, which was what happened to a passenger boat, which overturned in the Goring flash in 1634, with the loss of over sixty lives. Leave the run too late, however, and there was then a danger of grounding.

The biggest problem of all was administration – or, rather, the lack of it. The weirs were built and owned by the millers, and it was they who controlled the opening and closing of the flash locks. Opening a lock took water away from the mill, so they preferred to wait, sometimes for days, until there were enough boats collected together to make it worth their while. The boat owners, needless to say, paid tolls for the privilege of using the locks. In time, as river trade increased, the delays and dangers of the flash locks became ever more irksome. John Taylor, born in Gloucester in 1580, moved to London where he became a waterman, the 16th century equivalent of a London cabby, ferrying passengers along and over the Thames. In 1632 he described a trip that he made down the Thames, in verse. What set him apart from earlier commentators on the river was that he wrote as a practical waterman, describing just what it was like to travel by boat. Or, as he put it:

*As they before these Rivers bounds did show*
*Here I come after with my Pen and row.*

What he saw, he observed with the eye of experience and nothing infuriated him more than the actions of millers who prevented the free flow of river traffic.

*Shall private persons for their gainfull use,*
*Ingrosse the water and the land abuse,*
*Shall that which God and nature gives us free,*
*For use and profit in community,*
*Be barr'd from men, and damb'd up as in Thames,*
*(A shameless avarice surpassing shames;)*

As well as the general condemnations, he noted all the particular faults, all the problems he encountered. In theory, the flashes allowed boats to pass over the shallows, so that there was no need for dredging. It did not always work.

*At Clifton there are rocks, and sands, and flats,*
*Which made us wade, and wet like drowned rats.*

*A typical lock on the River Nene. The upper gates are the conventional mitre gates, but the bottom guillotine gate is a modern version of the type that has been in use since the Middle Ages. This is raised and lowered by means of the crank that can be seen on the right of the frame.*

Astonishingly, this very much less than satisfactory device remained in use on the Thames until well into the 20th century. The very last flash lock was only removed from the upper river at Eynsham in 1931, and a few were still to be found on backwaters even after that date.

Nearly half a century later, things were little better. In 1670, Sir Christopher Wren wrote a report on the state of the River Lea, investigating complaints made by the 'Inhabitants and bargemen belonging to the towns of Hereford and Ware.' One particularly pernicious custom was that of the millers charging the boat owners for the use of the flash, then closing it prematurely and drawing off extra water so that the vessels were quickly grounded. The millers then demanded a second fee to float them off again. 'It is certain that some of the mills do so command the Streams, that they can lay a whole fleet of Barges on ground upon the adjoining sharps and help them off again upon Composition.' Wren's solution was one that was being increasingly used on Britain's rivers. He recommended appointing a regulatory body, or 'Commission of Sewers' to make sure the flashes were correctly used and prices were reasonable. Such bodies also began the essential work of making genuine river improvements.

The flashes have gone, though remains can still be seen at various places, for example immediately downstream of Jubilee Bridge at Fladbury on the

The most common method of allowing water in and out of a lock is by means of a culvert, closed by a cover or paddle that is raised vertically. Here the typical paddle gear is shown, where movement is via a ratchet worked by a simple windlass. In the first picture the gear is down and the culvert is closed. In the second the ratchet is raised and held in place by a catch to stop it slipping.

Warwickshire Avon. Yet, even in Taylor's day the river was changing, with the construction of what he referred to as 'turnpikes' but which we know as pound locks or simply as locks. The story of how the pound lock developed takes us away from the millers and out of Britain.

The main centre for canal development in medieval Europe was the Netherlands. History may be vague on whether or not the Romans used their drainage canals for transport, but we certainly know that the Dutch did. The main drainage canals were linked to rivers and estuaries by dykes, with the flow of water between them controlled by sluices. These were generally of the portcullis type, in which the controlling gate was raised and lowered vertically in a fixed frame. An obvious next step was to make a portcullis sluice that would be big enough to allow boats to pass from one water system to the other when water levels were equal, for example between canal and estuarial river at the appropriate state of the tide. Such large gates required considerable engineering works to ensure a watertight fit. It became practice to extend the abutments of a portcullis lock out into the banks and to protect the foundations with sheet piling. The pile driver was probably the first machine

*The wide lock connecting the Exeter Ship Canal to the river Exe, here seen at low tide. Originally built in the seventeenth century, the canal has been transformed over the years, with major improvements in the nineteenth century. The original lock was turf-sided, but the present structure is still known as Turf Lock.*

to be introduced into the world of canal engineering. The earlier versions looked, and worked, rather like the later guillotine. A heavy weight was raised between vertical guides using a simple crank. When it reached the top of the frame, a release mechanism allowed it to drop back onto the top of the pile. Pile drivers could also be mounted on barges, and the larger engines used a treadmill instead of a hand crank to raise the weight.

The next important change came in the late 14th century, when engineers began setting sluices close together, creating what were in effect tide locks. When conditions were right, the outer gate was raised and vessels could leave the tideway and enter the basin. The outer gate was then closed and the inner gate was opened and, once levels had equalized, boats could move out onto the canal. Boats from the canal could now enter the basin, and the process was reversed. This system had a limited usefulness, but nothing more elaborate was needed in a country where water levels might vary but land levels remained conveniently flat. There was, however, an obvious next step, to use a similar system to overcome a river gradient, which seems to have been first tried on a short canal south of Lübeck in northern Germany.

The next steps were merely logical developments. One of the earliest illustrations of a lock from the 15th century shows two portcullis sluices set close together, but in between there is simply the river bank left in a natural state. From this crude beginning there was a progression to developing a lock chamber with a watertight lining, built to a size designed to fit the boats using that particular waterway. Most of these advances took place in Italy, where the last great improvement was made. The portcullis was a clumsy arrangement, and it was that universal genius Leonardo da Vinci who hit upon the idea of closing the lock off with a pair of gates meeting at an angle, as in a mitre joint, hence the name 'mitre gates'. The gates were angled to point upstream, so that the pressure of water always forced them together. The result can be seen in the great majority of locks that are in use today. It was time for Britain to start catching up with the rest of Europe.

One of the problems in looking for the forerunners of canals is that very few of the early structures have survived in anything resembling the form in which they were built. Even the river itself may have moved; the further back in time one looks, the more likely this is to have happened. A typical example can be seen at the point where Hadrian's Wall crosses the River Irthing near Birdoswald. The abutments of the bridge can still be seen, together with evidence of a water mill, but the river itself has gone wandering off in a wide loop leaving the ruins literally high and dry. There are, however, still places where, if one cannot see the original, one can at least get an idea of what the mechanisms of the early river navigations were like.

The River Nene retained its staunches until the late 1920s, and even after modernisation, the locks were fitted with portcullis or guillotine gates at their lower ends. These may be more sophisticated than their predecessors in many ways, but they can still demand a great deal of hard work from those who come this way by boat. Where the gates have to be raised by windlass, it can involve as many as 150 turns of the handle. It is not too surprising that these are rare survivors of an old tradition, for the first waterway to apply the new technology from the Netherlands and Italy was the Exeter Canal, built between 1564 and 1567.

The canal was designed by John Trew, of whom little is known other than that he was described as 'a gentleman from Glamorganshire'. It was, in effect, no more than a bypass for a particularly annoying obstruction – as far as the merchants of Exeter were concerned – that prevented vessels from reaching the city, namely the Countess Wear. As control of the weir rested in Topsham, which was a thriving port that had developed as the head of navigation, the Exeter boatmen could look for no help from that quarter. So it was that Trew set about creating a short, artificial cutting to take vessels round the Countess Wear. In many ways this was like the Dutch system, where the 'lock' was really a holding basin, 189ft long and 23ft wide, but it also used the new technology from Italy, with mitre gates at the upstream end, massive affairs with six sluices or paddles set into the gates. The lower end was closed by a single gate. The lock itself was built with turf sides, and although it has long since been replaced, the name 'Turf Lock' has survived for the lock linking the canal to the estuary. The canal was improved and lengthened at the end of the seventeenth century and again in the nineteenth, to reach its final form as the Exeter Ship Canal, a broad waterway stretching from the Exe to the heart of the city. The navigational features have altered out of all recognition, but one can still see some of the old buildings that grew up around the new inland port of Exeter.

One particularly fine survivor is the Custom House of 1681. It wears a proud air of prosperity, handsomely proportioned with a pediment displaying the coat of arms. A rather odd note is struck on the ground floor, with an array of arches that look fitting, but the windows in the recesses are out of scale with those of the floor above. They break with the conventional rules of architecture of the period, that window size should either remain uniform or should diminish with succeeding floors. Fortunately, we have an account of the building when it was new from an indomitable lady traveller, Celia Fiennes, who travelled around England on horseback and kept a diary of her journeys. In her day, the ground floor was entirely open to the quay and windowless, providing a dry area for storing goods. From here, external staircases led up to the first floor and to one grand room, partitioned into booths for the clerks and customs officers. The Custom House is a good indicator of the wealth created in Exeter by the construction of this one short canal, for it is as grand as could be found in any well established port.

The other indicator of the canal's success lies in its continuity of use, the fact that it was still worth spending a large amount of money on improvements two centuries after it was first built. James Green was the engineer who completed the final stage of development in the 1820s. He was responsible for the new tide lock at The Turf, for increasing the depth of the

*The Exeter Custom House of 1681, built at the city end of the Exeter Ship Canal. The arcade at ground level was originally open, with all the offices lit by the large windows on the floor above.*

canal to fifteen feet to accommodate the larger ships of the day and for constructing the new public wharf and warehouses at the Exeter end. Perhaps the most remarkable aspect of the Exeter scene is the clear sense of continuity from Quay House, built in the 1690s, through to the Wharfinger's Office, finished a century later, and on to the nineteenth century warehouses. There is also a clear theme developing that will recur throughout the canal story. These are all practical buildings, where there is a close and obvious correlation between outward form and use. So, while the Custom House has an elegant refinement that sits comfortably with its role as representing the majesty of the law and the dignity of the crown, the warehouses are solidly practical, built of massive sandstone blocks that positively proclaim the message that anything entrusted to them would be kept secure. The men who built the warehouses were well aware that they were there to be used in a rough, commercial world. When we look at them today, it is no good expecting to find delicate ornamentation and refined detailing. What one does find is a robust simplicity that is visually satisfying and even exciting. The random rubble walls, with blocks of a rich variety of shapes and sizes, provide one kind of pattern, which contrasts with the huge, roughly dressed quoins and the sturdy arches over doorways with their prominent keystones. Again the irregularity of the individual stones contrasts with the regular rhythm of the façade, with its uniform arrays of windows and loading bays.

*The quayside at Exeter with its robust stone warehouses, when it was home to the maritime museum. Among the vessels on show is Brunel's steam dredger* Bertha, *easily recognized by its tall black funnel.*

In assessing the quality of buildings such as these, it is necessary to know just how they were to be used. The interiors of the warehouses are even more plain than the outsides, with rough walls and exposed beams and no attempt to define particular spaces very closely. This fits perfectly with the way in which they functioned, for they would have been home to a huge array of very different goods. There is a hint of what they were expected to hold in the nineteenth century act of parliament, which established the tolls to be paid on different classes of goods. Over 300 different items are listed, starting at alum and ending at yarn wick, and in between everything from that most important of West Country commodities, bales of wool, to the domestic trivia of frying pans. Given such diversity of merchandise, the need for totally flexible space becomes clear. The other message that comes across very clearly at Exeter is the commercial importance of a waterway such as the Exeter Canal in its own day.

It is quite difficult today to form a concept of the extent to which rivers were used in the years before the start of the canal age, just how many waterways were busy with trade that would now seem quite impassable. The River Wye is a particularly good example; now scarcely used by anything bigger than a canoe, it was once a very important navigation. The opening of the Wye Valley Railway in 1876 began a period of rapid decline in river traffic, but barges still kept on trading as high as Bigsweir Bridge as late as the 1920s. There are remains of wharves at various points on the way upstream and many indications of what was once a busy industrial scene. Tintern is now famous for the romantic abbey ruins, but it was once busy with wireworks and quays; a slipway and a possible boatyard site can still be identified. More impressive still are the remains at Redbrook. Copper ore was brought by water from Cornwall via Chepstow and smelted with coal from the mines of the Forest of Dean. This lasted until the 1740s, and the same site was later developed as a tinplate works. An old warehouse on the quay survives from this time of busy industrial activity.

The story continues all the way to Hereford, where Quay Street still leads down to the river, though the quay itself has long gone, and the old coal wharves can be seen close to Wye Bridge. There is even one reminder of the type of vessels that plied the river, and just how far they traded. The Sloop Inn at Llandogo still has the bell of the last ship to sail this far upstream, the *William and Sarah*, and it can be matched with a quayside pub in Bristol docks, the Llandoger Trow. The trow was the transom-sterned sailing barge that worked the Severn, Wye and Avon. Even more remarkable than this story of the busy life of the Wye is the fact that the little tributary, the Lugg, which joins the main river at Mordiford, was also navigable. There is a record that the bells of Leominster Priory were sent by barge to Chepstow for recasting in 1750. Here the river was controlled by flash locks, and the somewhat crumbling remains can be seen just upstream of Mordiford Bridge.

Other navigations have never fallen out of use and still have structures in place, but on the busiest, such as the Rivers Thames and Severn, modernisation has drastically changed the riverscape. Even here, however, there are memories of old days and old working practices. Long distance walkers now use the former towpaths, along which, in the days before engines, men used to make their way hauling the heavy barges behind them – human haulage was as common as haulage by horse on both these rivers. But to get a clearer idea of how engineers set about river improvement in the years leading up to the canal age one has to look elsewhere.

Some of the most interesting examples of early navigational works can be found on the River Kennet. The engineer was John Hore, whose family were local maltsters in Newbury, at what was to become the western terminus of the new navigation. Quite where he attained his engineering skills is unknown, but those skills were sorely tested, for the natural river was not to be easily tamed, with a fall of 138ft from Newbury down to the Thames at Reading. Work began in 1718 and continued for the next five years. Such a large drop required no fewer than eighteen locks, which had to be big enough to take the large West Country barges which were already in use in the region. These were very different from the famous sailing barges of the tidal Thames. They were blunt, rudimentary vessels, with a small foredeck carrying a winch and an anchor, a large open hold, and a small cabin or simple canvas awning by the steering position at the stern. There was a single mast to which the tow rope was attached, and from which a small square sail could be hoisted in favourable conditions. The most common barges were approximately sixty-five feet long and had a ten-foot beam, but there were also a few that were almost twice as long, vessels that carried an impressive 170 tons. It was decided that the Kennet locks should accommodate the biggest of the craft.

It is not possible to build locks stretching across the river from bank to bank. If this were done, they would simply act as dams when not in use. There has to be an arrangement for allowing water to flow regardless of traffic. The standard solution was to build a weir across the whole river but, instead of setting a lock in the middle, as with the old flash locks, an artificial cutting was dug from a point well above the weir to a point well below it, and in this cutting the lock could be built. With a river having such a severe gradient as

*Building conventional bridges across a broad waterway was an expensive business, so wherever possible the engineers on the Kennet Navigation used swing bridges, pivoting in a stone-lined recess. This bridge, being closed behind the passing boat, is at Ufton.*

the Kennet, the length of these artificial cuttings was increased to avoid rapids and shallows. In the eighteen-mile length of the whole navigation, no fewer than eleven miles are in artificial cutting. This presented the engineers with some new problems. The river had flowed through the land before man ever settled it, and communities had grown up which had accepted it as a natural barrier, defining boundaries. But the new lateral cuts sliced right through the old divisions, and landowners, not unreasonably, took a dim view of having one part of their property separated from the other part by a fifty-four foot wide waterway. The navigation authorities had to satisfy their demands by building accommodation bridges. There was nothing new about building bridges over rivers, but in the past they had appeared at infrequent intervals at major crossing points. But now there were not only a lot more to be built, but they had to be built so as not to obstruct the boats. The expense of constructing a whole series of high arched bridges in brick and stone was simply too great, so Hore went for the other option, movable bridges. The Kennet swing bridges have a pivotal point on a turntable set on one bank and simple timber decking. Although cheaper to construct, they prove far more troublesome over the years, as the weight of the deck causes the ends to droop and sag. Instead of moving smoothly in their stone-lined recesses, they drag and catch. There was just one stone bridge constructed at Burghfield.

The most important decision the engineer had to face was how he was to construct the locks. Hore followed the precedents set on such early waterways as the Exeter Canal, and relied mainly on turf locks. These were built with sloping earth sides, bound together as the name suggests by grass. Masonry was limited to the abutments for lock gates, though further strengthening was supplied by timber linings to the lower part of the lock chamber. No working locks now survive as built, but one example of a lock chamber has been preserved at Monkey Marsh. Beneath the water line, the timber sides rise to a height of two feet, while above that the sides spread out at an angle of 45° – anything steeper than that would be liable to collapse. The guard rails are a comparatively recent addition, added when the canal was in the ownership of the Great Western Railway. An alternative to timbering was a lining of brick or stone. There was no suitable stone in the area and transport costs overland were high – which was why so much money was being spent on the river in the first place. So although brick looked like the only option, there were grave doubts about a brick chamber being able to withstand the pressure from the surrounding ground. An arch is better able to stand the strain than a straight wall, so that when the decision was taken to reduce the size of the locks by shortening them and building a new brick chamber inside the old turf one, the walls were built in a scallop shape, with a series of small arches when seen on plan. There is a splendid example still to be seen at Aldermaston.

Like all the old navigations, the Kennet has seen immense changes over the years, but enough remains to give us a very good idea of the thinking that went into its construction. Many tough problems were solved, but it was still tied to the

*Garston turf lock on the Kennet. The water has risen up the sloping turf sides, but in modern usage only the central section between the guides is used by boats, hence the short bridge to the steps.*

river. It was the river that provided the water, and the lateral cuts never strayed far from their source. There was no need for the cutting to cross the river or join it other than on the level. Water supply was not an issue: if there was not enough water in the Kennet to fill the cuts then that was unfortunate, but the river would itself be unnavigable, so there was nothing to be done. As time went on, engineers found themselves facing ever more intractable rivers, and the proportion of artificial cutting in the finished navigation rose steadily. Then in 1755, work began on what was known as the Sankey Brook. Although the navigation followed the line of the brook it was now entirely in man made cutting, and was eventually given a more appropriate name, the St Helen's Canal.

To many historians, this was England's first true canal, but it did not seem so at the time. It was perceived as no more than an extreme example of a river navigation, even though the 'river' was capable of taking nothing much bigger than a toy boat. It was the Bridgewater Canal, begun just five years later, that was to be hailed as the true original and which was to inaugurate the canal age in a burst of wild enthusiasm. It was not so much that the Bridgewater was different from anything that had gone before, but it was perceived as being different. Where the St. Helen's Canal trotted amicably along beside the modest wanderings of the Sankey Brook, the Bridgewater went boldly off on its own way, leaping right over the mighty River Irwell on the imposing Barton aqueduct. Here, it seemed, was something really new and crowds gathered to marvel at the sight of boats on a waterway high in the air crossing above other boats on the older navigation. It was a potent symbol of a new era. But was it really a new occurrence? Only when seen by those who had not looked at what was happening across the English Channel. Compared with what had already been achieved in France, the Bridgewater Canal was puny and, for all the claims made for it by its admirers, it was France that had inspired the English work. Its promoter and financier, Francis Egerton, third Duke of Bridgewater, had as many young noblemen before him, set off to complete his education on the Grand Tour of Europe. He gazed at art and antiquities, filled packing cases with busts and statues, and promptly forgot them. The cases were never unpacked, the busts never set on their pedestals.

*Some early locks on the Kennet were given a brick lining, and Aldermaston lock has a curious scalloped edge. This was not a decorative effect: by using a series of arches the builders produced a structure better able to withstand pressure than a straight wall.*

*Long before any true canal had been built in Britain, Pierre-Paul Riquet was at work on the Canal du Midi in France. Construction began in 1666 and included this spectacular seven-lock staircase at Fonserannes* (A.Burton).

What excited the Duke was not the past world of Greece and Rome but the future world exemplified by the Canal du Midi.

The idea of a canal that would link the Atlantic to the Mediterranean was not new, and had been seriously discussed as early as the sixteenth century. But all schemes foundered on the vexed problem of how to provide sufficient water for a 'summit canal', one that had to cross over a watershed. If water could not be fed into the highest level of the canal, then it would rapidly be drained down as locks full of water were pulled off. This was not a problem on the older navigations, which kept pace with the rivers. It was Pierre-Paul Riquet, not an engineer but a man who made his money collecting the salt tax, who found the answer. There was abundant water in the Montagne Noir region, but to be of any use it would have to be collected in one or more reservoirs then channelled down to the watershed, a point that needed to be located, from which water flowed in two directions – to the river systems of the Atlantic or to those of the Mediterranean. The system of reservoirs and their associated *rigoles*, or water channels, was as complex as that of many a navigable canal. The first part to be completed, after work began in 1666, was the Rigole de la Montagne, a channel that ran for twenty-five kilometres (sixteen miles) to the summit level of the canal. But by far the most impressive work was the great Saint-Ferréol reservoir. The retaining wall was built of

*The Canal du Midi boasts the world's first canal tunnel at Malpas. As the illustration shows, it was hacked through the soft rock, which has been honeycombed by erosion* (A. Burton).

earth banks with a substantial masonry core. The length at the top was 786m (2580ft) and at its base, the earth bank reached a width of 149m (488 ft). The water pressure exerted against the dam is immense, and visitors can see just how powerful it is when a controlled amount of water is allowed to vent through a pipe at the foot of the dam, sending a plume of water high in the air as an ornamental fountain. All these truly great works were simply there to supply the water to keep the canal open.

In designing the canal structures themselves, Riquet was no less daring. Not content with building locks, he ran them together, so that the top gates of the lower lock were also the bottom gates of the one above, creating a watery staircase. When completed, the Canal du Midi had ninety-two locks – forty-five single, twelve double, four triple, one quadruple and, grandest of them all, a staircase of seven interconnected locks at Fonserannes. All were built on a grand scale, with chambers 30m long and 5.6m wide (98ft by 18ft). Riquet encountered problems right at the beginning of construction, however, when earth movement caused one of the locks to collapse. He promptly set about redesigning them all. His solution was, as on the Kennet, to utilize the strength of the arch, by building each lock with a distinctive oval chamber. There were two other problems, which had not been faced by the engineers of the river navigations – how to cope with rivers and ridges running across the line of the canal. The easiest way to deal with the former was to cross at the level, and with minor streams to culvert them under the canal. This was not possible with big rivers, so Riquet had to build aqueducts, the grandest of which across the Répudre has a central span of ten metres (thirty-three feet). It was constructed out of two layers of dressed stone, closely keyed together, with a central coarse filling. The other obstacle to be overcome was the hilly country that he called his 'bad step' – *malpas*. Here he had to tunnel through the rock for 165m (541ft).

The tunnel itself was built to generous dimensions, 7.3m (24ft) wide, with the crown of the arch 5.8m (19ft) above water level. Fortunately for Riquet, the sandstone was easily worked, and one can see at the western end that natural erosion has created a honeycomb effect. It remains, however, an imposing first in canal engineering, and those dimensions should be kept in mind when it comes to assessing what British engineers achieved a century later.

This was the canal that so impressed the seventeen-year-old Duke of Bridgewater when he visited it in 1753. Just five years later he was beginning to plan for a canal of his own. The idea was born in France, but unfortunately the engineers who were to make his plans a reality and start the canal revolution had never left England. They were about to reinvent the wheel.

# 2. The Bridgewater Story

The importance of the Bridgewater initiative has already been stressed, and now it is time to look at the enterprise in more detail. When the young Duke of Bridgewater turned his back on the social life of London, embittered, it was said, by an unhappy affair of the heart, he turned all his energies into developing the mines on his estate. Mineral rights were an important source of revenue for many aristocratic families, but few did more than farm the work out to professionals and pocket the profits. The Duke was different. He was personally involved, the true driving force behind the enterprise of modernizing and increasing the profitability of the mines. He also had a most enthusiastic and able helper in his land agent, John Gilbert. Together they began to lay plans for a canal, but one with origins very different from those of the vast majority of other canals: those origins lay deep underground.

The coal mines of Worsley Delph were like many other mines, damp, dripping places, and as the miners advanced and went ever deeper, they often encountered springs that hampered progress. There are two basic methods of getting water out of mines, by pumping or by draining, through an adit or sough. The planners had a brilliant idea. An adit would be built, tunneling deep into the hillside, but it would not be used simply as a massive drain. Boats could float along it, right up to the coal face for loading. Then, once the adit had reached the open air, the water would not be allowed simply to flow away into the nearest stream. It would be used to fill a canal that would carry the boats on their way along this brand new, navigable waterway to the rapidly growing town of Manchester. This meant that fuel could be delivered directly from coal face to customer by the cheapest means of transport then available. It would be a very efficient system, and if everything went to plan it would slash costs dramatically. The water that was such a nuisance to the miners was to be a boon to the canal builders; it would keep the waterway permanently filled, without the expense of constructing reservoirs.

In 1759, plans were submitted to parliament and an Act obtained for a canal that would follow a contour at around the eighty-foot level from Worsley to Salford, keeping all the time to the north of the Irwell. Work began at once, with Gilbert as the man in charge, doubly qualified for the task as both an experienced mining engineer and a land agent, the latter job involving the essential skills of surveying. Work went on simultaneously in tunnelling through the hill and in constructing the broad waterway of the canal proper. Not much progress had been made before plans were changed, and an altogether more ambitious scheme was put forward. The main canal was now to head for the very heart of Manchester itself, and there was a new long-term objective of creating a waterway that would link the town to Liverpool and the Mersey. The planners had also accepted a daunting challenge: they would now have to cross the River Irwell on an aqueduct and, because the river was navigable, it would have to be built high enough to allow tall-masted sailing barges to pass underneath. A new name then appeared on the team: James Brindley was a Derbyshire millwright with a reputation as an ingenious mechanic and a man unafraid of new ideas.

It is difficult to apportion credit for the Bridgewater Canal between the three protagonists, but roughly speaking one can think of the Duke as the promoter, the man who footed the bills, Brindley as the chief engineer, responsible for the overall planning and Gilbert as the resident engineer, the man on the spot, solving problems as they arose. Even this broad generalization is open to question. In practice, the three met regularly to discuss all the problems and plans, and as no notes were taken we will never know who came up with which idea. One thing, however, is clear. The canal was a resounding success. Sadly, much of the most exciting and innovative work has either been lost or is hidden away from view, deep underground.

The obvious starting point for looking at the canal today is the entrance to the mines at Worsley Delph. There are two entrances that can be seen at the foot of the cliffs just to the north of the A574 in Worsley, where there is a wide basin stained a startlingly bright orange by iron ore from the mines. A clue as to what went on behind the openings can be seen in the form of a small, open boat, lying in the silt. It is a very simple affair: double-ended, with planking fastened to prominent, exposed ribs, which have given such vessels the name 'starvationer'. The starvationers were the vessels of the underground canal system. The vessels were not filled directly with coal, but with containers that were filled at the face and were specially designed to fit snugly into the open hulls. Once the boats were out in the open basin, five or six of them could be fastened together and towed off to Manchester by horse or mule. Today one gets no idea of the huge extent of the underground system, which lies behind the low, modest openings. In its final form, the underground canal system stretched for forty-six miles, made up of canals and branches at more than one level, the different levels linked by vertical shafts down which the coal containers could be raised and lowered. If the underground system is lost from sight, we do at least have a notion of how the basin looked in its working days. An illustration of 1770 shows that the wharf was then dominated by a massive swivel crane. If the artist has got his proportions right, which is a very big if, then it rose to a height of about forty feet.

From the mine entrance a now derelict canal leads to a much larger basin, with a long wharf area, from which broad steps rise up to a handsome eighteenth-century house, to which later, fashionable 'black-and-white' additions have given a romantic, old world appearance. It is an important

*The Packet House at Worsley. The modern equivalent of the old packet boat stands at the foot of the steps first used by passengers over two centuries ago. The modern boat, a converted working narrow boat, is very different from its purpose-built eighteenth-century predecessor.*

building in the canal story, for this is the Packet House, the hotel or inn from which passengers could join the packet boats for Manchester. This service was begun by the Duke in 1766 with two boats, one holding eighty, the other 120 passengers in 1st, 2nd and 3rd class accommodation, and serving refreshments en route. Passenger services were never as important as cargo carrying for the canal system, but they brought in a substantial revenue for the Duke, and survived for many years. Across the water is an old boatyard and dry dock, but little now remains to suggest that this was once the heart of a bustling, industrial community that grew up round the canal with lime kilns, brickworks, a pencil factory and numerous warehouses.

From here the canal continues as a broad, lock-free waterway heading for the site of its most famous structure, the aqueduct across the River Irwell at Barton. Contemporaries marvelled at this watery bridge, but quite failed to notice the vast embankments that led up to the river crossing. The bank to the north, faced with

*The famous Barton aqueduct photographed shortly before its demolition early in the 1890s when work began on the Manchester Ship Canal. The men look down from the Bridgewater Canal to a flat being towed along the Irwell.*

stone, was pierced by a short tunnel to carry the Eccles road. As many a canal engineer was to discover through the years, the building and stabilization of embankments could prove every bit as troublesome as the construction of aqueducts, and the Barton banks remain very impressive features. Visitors who arrive by land can climb the bank by steps at the southern end to get a true impression of how it strides across the landscape. But the two high embankments are no longer linked by a masonry aqueduct. The original aqueduct was demolished when the Irwell was swallowed up in the construction of the Manchester Ship Canal, to be replaced by the present swing aqueduct, and now all that remains of the original are the stone abutments. The large shaped blocks that still stand do at least give some impression of the size and strength of the old aqueduct. Fortunately, the original did survive long enough to reach into the age of photography, so we have a rather more reliable picture of what it really looked like than we might have had from any of the many rather fanciful pictures produced when it was new. There were two broad arches covering the Irwell Navigation and its towpath, and a narrower relieving arch. The photographs also show very clearly how what was otherwise a very conventional bridge of the period, with its segmented arches and prominent cutwaters, was converted into a structure that could carry a canal. Earth was piled above the masonry and can be seen as bound together by grass, which rises high above the parapet. Into this earth the canal channel was cut and lined with puddled clay. Once the water was admitted, it all represented a very heavy load, and at the first test there were ominous signs that one of the arches was collapsing. The danger turned out to be caused, ironically, by the overcautious approach of the engineers who had added far more heavy puddle than was necessary. Once some of that was removed, all was well. On 17 July 1761, the first flat, the traditional sailing barge of the Mersey, was towed across, providing the unique sight of one barge on the new canal sailing thiry-nine feet above another barge down on the Irwell. The aqueduct had a double importance. It was an imposing structure and looked reassuringly solid, but the early alarms meant that Brindley made doubly sure of the strength of his masonry on subsequent aqueducts, as we shall see later. Most importantly, it caught the public imagination, and did an enormous amount to engender enthusiasm for canal construction in the population at large. It has to be said, however, that a rather stronger impetus came from the halving of coal prices in Manchester once the whole canal was open, not to mention the considerable profits enjoyed by the Duke.

Equally impressive in its own way was the terminus at Castlefield in Manchester, under the bluff on which the Romans had built their castle. Sadly, once again the main features are gone. The basin was excavated and incorporated the River Medlock, with water controlled through an unusual clover-leaf patterned weir. This was considered a very attractive feature, but soon turned out to be quite impractical, frequently silting up.

Numerous warehouses were added over the years, but the most striking feature was the mechanism for unloading the coal. The boats from the mine were floated in underneath a shaft, and their containers were lifted by a hoist powered by a water wheel and raised to street level. The Castlefield of today bears very little resemblance to the Castlefield of the 1760s, having been changed forever by the arrival of later canals and the railway system of the nineteenth century.

As the first Bridgewater Canal opened for business in 1761, work was still proceeding on the extension to the Mersey at Runcorn. Once again there was to be a deviation from the route as first planned, thanks to the promotion of another, even grander, canal scheme – the Trent & Mersey. The Bridgewater could no longer be thought of in isolation, but now had to be seen as a vital link in a cross country route that was to join those two great rivers to create a navigation that would stretch from coast to coast. A meeting point for the two canals was soon fixed at Preston Brook, five miles from Runcorn. The two canals met end to end, through a one-mile long branch from the Bridgewater. In a sense, Brindley and Gilbert were fortunate in that the new canal lay across very flat country, while the two river crossings, of the Mersey and the Bollin, were over unnavigable reaches, so there was no need to supply the height needed at Barton. However, flat land is all too often boggy and marshy, and this was no exception. In crossing the flat land in the flood plain of the infant Mersey, an area then known as Sale Moor, the engineers were unable to follow the normal practice of digging a trench and puddling it, for the oozy mud simply slid back in again. Brindley devised a system of first digging trenches to hold timber balks which were fastened together to make continuous walls, and then packed with earth and clay to create a firm, watertight channel. This was an ingenious solution, but there is little to detect today, and extensive land drainage has quite changed the nature of the surrounding land. Very much more obvious are the embankments that stretch away to either side of the Bollin crossing on the edge of Dunham Park. The other major embankment over the Mersey can no longer be seen in isolation, following the construction of the adjoining railway. However, it is for the latter that we have contemporary statistics. Joseph Priestley's *Navigable Rivers and Canals* of 1831 describes it as being '900 yards long, 17 feet high and 112 feet at the base'. These are very considerable dimensions for what was, after all, a pioneering exercise in this form of construction. Although these banks are very much as they were, the abutments and aqueduct were replaced by concrete and sheet metal piling following a collapse in 1971.

The most important engineering work on the whole canal was the flight of locks joining it to the River Mersey at Runcorn. This was not completed until 1773, by which time the engineer, James Brindley, was dead. The locks were designed to allow the flats that were already trading in large numbers on the Mersey and the Weaver to use the new canal, and the dimensions were generous, 72ft long by 14ft 9in. beam. They were not the biggest locks to be built on a British navigation, but they were perfectly adequate to meet any conceivable demands for many years to come. Possibly the Duke had remembered what he had seen on his visit to the Canal du Midi, for the arrangement of the locks borrowed a notion from France. Instead of being built individually, the ten locks were arranged in connecting pairs. The average fall was seven feet, but the final drop could be as much as 22ft, so that boats could come and go, even at low tide. Like so much else on the Bridgewater, the old locks were superseded by later developments with the arrival of the Manchester Ship Canal. They are all now derelict, and the canal comes to a dead end.

There was to be one further development in this first stage in the life of the Bridgewater Canal: the construction of docks and warehouses on the Mersey, to allow for trans-shipment of goods. The Duke acquired land immediately to the west of the Salthouse Dock, close to what was to become the site of the Albert Dock. It was originally very modest, little more than an inlet from the river, contained within sandstone walls, and reached via a tidal lock. This led into a small, rectangular basin, approximately 200ft by 100ft, which became known as The Duke's Dock. This was opened in 1773, but the first warehouse on the Liverpool waterfront was not built until 1783, though more were to follow as trade increased. As with his canal, the Duke's Dock was overtaken by later developments. It suffered from its inconveniently narrow entrance, which made for an awkward connection with the river. This was eventually closed off, after which the only approach was through the larger Salthouse Dock. It remains, however, of considerable historical importance in the development of both the whole Liverpool dock complex and the inland waterway system. The closed-off inlet can be seen immediately downstream of the Albert Dock, leading into the basin by the road. Pleasure dinghies now sail where barges and flats once loaded and unloaded at the quayside.

The construction of the Bridgewater involved the building of numerous bridges which, unlike those of the Kennet, were fixed and built mainly of brick. A useful innovation was the provision of stop planks, which could be fitted into grooves in the canal bank to isolate a section for maintenance work and repairs. These became standard features on later canals. The other interesting feature of construction is the actual line along which the canal was built. The two canals run for over thirty miles on the level, without a single lock and with no major earthworks, apart from those required for river crossings. It is not easy to see on the ground just how this was achieved, but it all becomes clear when the line of the canal is traced across an Ordnance Survey map, when the canal appears as a blue line closely following the wanderings of the brown contour lines. This makes it all seem very easy, but one has to remember that Gilbert and Brindley did not have the benefit of any such maps, and had to make their own surveys and draw their own plans. A clear example of what came to be known as contour cutting can be seen on O.S. Landranger Sheet 109. The line of the canal from Lymm on its way past Warrington wriggles and squirms much as a river or stream would do, because all the time it is mimicking the twists and turns of the thirty metre contour on the map. It represents a clear choice: to accept the vagaries of the line

*The long straight line of the Bridgewater Canal as it crosses the flat land of what was once Sale Moor. The former wharf area has been restored, but perversely supplied with railings that make it unusable by boats.*

and the longer distance travelled, rather than go to the trouble and expense of building banks and digging cuttings. The engineers would certainly have preferred a direct line, and when the chance presented itself on the very flat land over Sale Moor, they took a totally arrow-straight course. Whichever of the planners of this early canal decided that contour cutting was far preferable, it was to be James Brindley who was to embrace the notion with enthusiasm and make it into the hallmark of all his later canals.

There has been a great deal of speculation about the building of the two Bridgewater canals, and there is one hypothesis which, though it cannot be proved, has gained wide acceptance – that a good deal of the fundamental design was the work of John Gilbert, even though Brindley was given much of the credit at the time. There is a reasonable explanation for this. Gilbert was employed directly by the Duke, and was happy to stay with him, working on his many and varied interests. He had no wish to act as engineer for anyone else's canal. Brindley's situation was very different. He was an entirely independent consultant, and having his name attached to the most famous waterway in Britain was the best advertisement that his skills could have. The work duly rolled in, but now Brindley was entirely his own master. Whether the work on the other canals that followed quickly on the heels of the Bridgewater would have been carried out in a different way if Gilbert had still been at Brindley's elbow is a question that can never be answered. What we can see is what Brindley learned from the Bridgewater, and how he applied those lessons on his later canals.

# 3. The Grand Trunk

The first major scheme to follow up the success of the Bridgewater Canal was the Trent & Mersey, promoted with great enthusiasm by the potter, Josiah Wedgwood. It is not difficult to see why he should have been so enthusiastic. His pottery was being developed using raw materials, such as flint, which had to be shipped round the coast and then sent overland at great expense. And the notion of sending cases of fragile pottery on a smooth canal rather than an atrocious, rutted road must have been particularly attractive. He was already aware of Brindley's abilities, as in his earlier career as a millwright the engineer had built a very successful flint-grinding mill for the Wedgwoods. So, in 1766, the new canal received its official act of parliament and work could go ahead, with Brindley as the man in charge. The Bridgewater interests were also well represented, for the canal provided an obvious means for the duke to extend his commercial ventures. There were high expectations of a speedy conclusion – expectations that were to be utterly unfulfilled.

The canal was built to a scale previously unknown in Britain, with a total length of over ninety-three miles, which earned it the name The Grand Trunk. It was to have a direct connection with the Trent at Derwent Mouth, but the Mersey connection was made via the link to the Bridgewater at Preston Brook, as described in the previous chapter. The Bridgewater had been specifically engineered to take Mersey flats, and it would have been a logical step to build the new canal to the same dimensions. This would have been equally useful at the other end of the canal. The Trent was used by vessels based on the Humber keels, blunt-bowed, carrying a square sail on a single mast, and they too could have been accommodated in the same sized locks as those which James Brindley was already building with Gilbert at Runcorn. But Gilbert was the Duke's man, and though there was a strong financial interest in the Trent & Mersey, there was no question of involvement in the actual engineering. So Brindley now had to take the decisions. The first six locks from the Trent to Horninglow Wharf, on the outskirts of Burton-on-Trent, were indeed built to take vessels up to 72ft long and 13ft 6in beam.

Had the canal been continued to the same standard, then Britain would have had a greatly different canal system, but Brindley had a major problem to overcome. He had to cross the watershed between two river systems, leaving the Trent valley for the Cheshire rivers, Dane and Weaver. Contour cutting could get him round most obstacles, but was no help at the summit. The ridge between the two river systems was too high to be crossed by locks, for it would have been quite impossible to find enough water to feed the summit. With no way round or over, the only alternative was to go through.

The route from the Trent was forced into convolutions as it wriggled its way through what is now Stoke-on-Trent. However, just to the north of Tunstall it came to Harecastle Hill, rising over a hundred feet above the line of the canal. This was far too high for Brindley to even consider open cutting, so now just one option remained – a tunnel. Surveys soon showed that it would have to be a very long tunnel, in fact 2,880 yards, over a mile and a half long. It would pass through an area of coal measures, so there was at least the possibility of following the example of Worsley, and using the tunnel to access possible new and profitable mines. Once again, any water drained from the mines could be used as a summit supply.

It was one thing to propose building a tunnel, but quite another to do so, for nothing on this scale had ever been attempted. It was quite obvious from tunnelling experience in the local collieries that much of the material through which the tunnel would be driven would not stand unsupported, so it would be

*When Brindley decided that locks on the Trent & Mersey should be half the width of those on the Bridgewater, a new type of cargo vessel had to be designed to fit them, the narrow boat. Here an old working boat is seen at Middlewich.*

necessary to construct a brick lining. If the tunnel was to be built wide enough to take the vessels that could use the locks at the Trent end, even if traffic was only one way, it would be necessary to have a bore that would allow for the brick lining and clear water on either side of the vessel. So Brindley was looking at the prospect of constructing a tunnel with a bore not less than sixteen feet in diameter through a hillside containing an unquantifiable mixture of hard rock, soft rock, quicksands and coal. There were no precedents for a transport tunnel of such a length, let alone one of such a large cross-section. He now had a canal that, up to that point, could take vessels of approximately 70ft by 16ft. Length was of no importance in the tunnel, and shaving a little off the width was no help – a 14ft-beam boat could no more go through a 13ft tunnel than it could one half as wide. And here was the obvious solution – to halve the width of the tunnel. This allowed efficient use of the wide locks, as two 7ft boats could fit in snugly, side by side. The saving in excavation would be immense. Because cross-section varies with the square of the radius, doubling the width quadruples the amount of material that has to be removed. It was a logical decision, but one with immense implications. There no longer seemed much point in going to the expense of building wide locks throughout the canal if wide boats were unable to pass through Harecastle. So locks were also reduced to accept boats roughly 7ft wide and 70ft long. Such boats did not exist, so they had to be built and were to become the most common vessels of the English canal system, the familiar narrow boats.

Brindley's determination to minimize excavation brought about a further saving when he decided that the tunnel would have no towpath. Once the dimensions had been fixed, work could begin. In order to construct the tunnel, the line had to be laid out on the surface. Standard surveying techniques, using theodolite and spirit level allowed altitudes to be measured above a base line. This meant that shafts could be sunk to a predetermined depth, and the tunnel extended out horizontally from the foot in two directions. Fifteen shafts were dug down through Harecastle Hill, providing thirty headings with two more from the mouths at either end. That meant that there were thirty-two groups of men all tunneling away and – in theory – all meeting up in a straight line.

In later years, engineers were highly critical of Brindley's work, but they wrote with the benefit of hindsight. When work began in 1766, the engineer had little or no notion of what he was to meet, for the science of geology was yet to be invented, but there was a general air of optimism. A contemporary wrote that Brindley 'handles rocks as easily as you would plum pies and makes the four elements subservient to his will'. And when sceptics questioned Brindley's ability to complete the work within the specified five years, he wagered £200 that it would be ready on time. He never had to pay up, for he was dead by the time it was finally opened in 1777, eleven years after work began.

Difficulties were far greater than had been anticipated. Problems with water in the tunnel were expected, but in the event the wind- and water-powered pumps that were meant to drain the workings proved inadequate, so a small steam pump had to be installed and kept running day and night. Far more serious was the varied

*The visual appeal of a canal lock is often a matter of pleasing contrasts. The angular black and white of the balance beam is set against the rounded edges of stone steps and the rough pattern of cobbles. The canal pub, the Star Inn at Stone, is a contemporary of the canal.*

nature of the material in the hill; that did indeed cover the whole range from hard rock to quicksand. Inside the tunnel, the bore was kept to a uniform size by the use of 'formers' of the correct profile, made of wood or iron. As the work advanced, the bricklayers followed on behind, building the lining to form a waterproof tube. In profile, it was semi-circular at the top, reaching down to a segmented arch at the bottom. Because strata were not understood, no one was aware that the different rock layers were inclined at an angle, so that water, rather than draining away vertically, tended to accumulate behind the brickwork, exerting a considerable pressure that was to cause trouble in the years to come. The bricks themselves were not specially selected for the job, but were fired on site using local clay.

When it was eventually opened, the tunnel proved to be far from straight, the different headings often meeting at awkward angles. The integrity of the whole structure was threatened by mining activity, with arches being struck through the tunnel walls to give easy access to the coal seams. It was unquestionably a bold endeavour for its time and the canal as a whole proved a great success. It was this success that showed up the shortcomings of the tunnel. As more and more traffic appeared on the waterway, so the delays became increasingly infuriating. As there was no towpath, boats had to be legged through by men lying on their backs and walking the boats along, pushing with their feet against the tunnel wall. It was a slow and laborious process, and as the tunnel was not wide enough for boats to pass, half the day was given over to northbound traffic, the other half to southbound. It was a bottleneck that needed to be unplugged.

It was soon generally agreed that Brindley's tunnel was less than perfect. John Rennie reported in 1822 that it was narrow, crooked and more worryingly, 'the brickwork which forms the bottom, sides and top of the Tunnel is not more than 9 inches thick, it has throughout been made with bad mortar, so that in all the brickwork under water the mortar is as soft as clay.' The solution was either to enlarge and improve the old tunnel or to build a new one. As the first option would have involved catastrophic disruptions to trade, the proprietors went for the second option. To save money, however, the new tunnel would again be narrow, but would have a towpath for greater efficiency. The old was to be repaired and patched up, so that there would then be two tunnels, each with one-way traffic. Given the reports on the Brindley tunnel, it looks like a classic case of short-term thinking and sure enough, in time the old tunnel did collapse and once again Harecastle had one single-bore tunnel.

The portals of the old tunnel can still be seen, but otherwise it is inaccessible. The new was begun in 1824 under the direction of Thomas Telford. It is an indication of how rapidly technology had moved on that where the old had taken eleven years to complete, the new with its wider bore to include a towpath was completed in three. This is the tunnel in use today, and it is as straight as its predecessor was crooked. Construction methods were similar to those of the first, but this time with seventeen shafts, linked above and below ground by railed tracks for greater efficiency. Steam pumps were used from the first, and a brickworks established that produced seven million bricks. These were flatter than the normal bricks, exceptionally hard and non-porous. It was well known that one problem in moving a boat through a narrow tunnel is the build up of water pressure ahead of the bows. Telford eased that problem by cantilevering the towpath out from the walls on iron brackets, with additional supports from place to place, so that water passed underneath the towpath, occupying the full width of the tunnel. The author was fortunate enough to be able to visit the tunnel when it was drained for repairs in 1977. Several of the old iron formers had been recovered and when offered up against the lining still showed a very good fit, showing how well the brickwork had survived a century and a half of use. A rather more alarming feature was the number of blocked up arches leading to the mines, and still leaching ochre into the water.

Over the years, improvements were made in the Telford tunnel. Poor ventilation meant that steam tugs could not be used, but in 1914 electric tugs were introduced. Initially, they were recharged at a generating station at the south end. Later an overhead cable and pick-up system was installed, similar to that used for the old tramcars. Then in 1954, fan ventilation was introduced and any powered craft could be used in the tunnel, which was an improvement but as the old tunnel had now been abandoned, one way working was in operation just as it had been in 1777. One can get little idea now of the inside of the Brindley tunnel, but there are three more long tunnels on the canal which remain in use – Saltersford (424 yards), Barnton (572 yards) and Preston Brook (1,239 yards). None has a towpath and all are noticeably crooked, and one can see how, wherever the rock was solid enough, the tunnels have been left unlined. The short Armitage tunnel is quite different, carved out of the natural rock and enjoying the luxury of a towpath. A great deal of space has been devoted to Harecastle because of its historic importance, for it effectively set the gauge for the whole Midland canal system, as surely as George Stephenson set the gauge for the railway system when he placed his rails 4ft 8½inches apart.

Turning to the canal as a whole, the most striking feature is the way in which it so closely mimics the line of the natural rivers. This is particularly noticeable in the section between Shardlow and the summit at Etruria. It begins quite promisingly, heading more or less west in the general direction of Stoke-on-Trent. Then it sways away with the river, turning south before heading back north in a great loop. A straight line route would have been forty-one miles long – the Trent valley line is fifty-seven miles, and required forty locks. So close are river and canal that at Alrewas they briefly converge, separating again by a large, open weir below the village. On this section, the towpath is carried on a low, trestle bridge to keep it clear of the flood plain.

On the whole, the structures along the canal are noted for their simplicity rather than elaboration, but are none the worse for that. Local materials are used, and as most of the route lies through land where good building stone is scarce but marl predominates, bricks were made in kilns set up close to the canal. The most prolific structures are the bridges, numbered from Shardlow and ending with No.213 at Preston Brook, and simply because there are so many they are easy to overlook. They just pass by, a succession of little hump-

*A classic scene at Tattenhall lock. A typical brick bridge, parapet and arch reinforced in stone, crosses the tail of the lock. The lock cottage is built in a vernacular style that was already familiar throughout the surrounding countryside, only distinguished by the windows in the gable end providing the view down the canal.*

backed blips on the skyline, with the occasional more imposing road bridge to add variety. Yet they merit a closer study. The first thing one notices is that the bricks from which they are built are quite unlike the modern machine bricks. They were cast in hand-made moulds and firing was never very closely controlled. The result is a pleasing slight irregularity in shape and size, and an even more delightful range of colours, where even the bricks of one bridge may vary from a deep blueish-red to an orangey-yellow. Because the bricks were seldom made very far from the place where they were to be used, the structures have an almost organic quality, seeming to grow out of the ground on which they stand

Brick on its own would not withstand the constant wear of tow-ropes, so the edges of the arch are lined with stone, which even then can be seen to be cut by deep grooves from years of use. The parapets are also protected by stone coping.

The actual design is also more complex than it at first appears. Firstly, when seen in plan, the bridge is not squared off but splayed out at the ends to support the approach road or track, and further strengthening is supplied by building the wing walls with a slight batter. Economy of materials was all important, so the size of the arch is reduced by pinching in the canal itself to a single boat's width, creating what generations of boaters have known as a 'bridge hole'. Wherever possible, they were built over the tail of a lock, taking advantage of the fall in ground to reduce the height that the bridge itself had to rise, while at the same time gaining extra strength from the wing walls of the lock.

*Wharves along the canal were a vital part of trade and at junctions could develop into small settlements. At Fradley Junction, where the Trent & Mersey meets the Coventry Canal, warehouse, inn and cottages blend harmoniously together.*

*Trent Corn Mill No.2 at Shardlow is an early example of a type of building that was to play a prominent role in canal architecture. It is built over a wide arch, or boat hole, allowing narrow boats and barges to load directly from the floor above.*

The work of the canal owners was not finished once the canal was open; it had to be run and maintained. The movement of boats needed to be controlled, repairs carried out and the tolls, the revenue which it was hoped would one day give the proprietors a handsome profit, had to be collected. So there was a need for lock cottages, toll-houses and maintenance depots. The cottages are generally very little different from those that might be built for farm workers, and could safely be trusted to the hands of local builders. Among the few distinctive features on some cottages were windows in the end walls to give the lock keeper a good view up and down the canal. Toll-houses and depots were, in general, purely functional on the Trent & Mersey, though there are some interesting variations on other early canals, which we shall look at later. The main business of the canal, however, was trade, and that meant the provision of wharves and warehouses, at regular intervals along the way. These were particularly important at Shardlow, where the old rivercraft met the new narrow boats and trans-shipment was often necessary. As a result, this became an important inland port, and although much has changed, enough remains to give a feel of what went on here. Some fine eighteenth century houses have survived, a sure indication that the canal brought prosperity, and the purely functional warehouses seem also to share something of the dignified simplicity of the domestic architecture. A fine red brick warehouse

*A canalside warehouse at Shardlow, with loading bays rising above the water. The small semi-circular windows with iron-glazing bars are an attractive feature, but crude conversion has destroyed the building's symmetry.*

by the wharf has a 'waggon corner', rounded off so that if a clumsy carter did allow his waggon to collide with it, the vehicle would simply glance off without causing very much damage.

In order to make full use of the site, the upper part of the wall is corbelled out so that the walls eventually meet at a conventional right angle. Built in 1799, it served the Shardlow Malt Extract Co., of which little now remains other than the name preserved in the nearby Malt Shovel Inn. Another warehouse from a slightly later period shows a typical arrangement of loading bays, one above the other, all served by the same hoist. It is less usual, in having an array of semi-circular windows in the gable end, with a fan pattern of iron glazing bars. The most interesting building in the complex is the Trent Corn Mills, No.2 Mill, a fine brick building dating from 1780 and built out on an arch over a spur of the canal. There is the usual array of loading bays for carts, but boats float right through the arch and under the building, where they can be loaded and unloaded in the dry through trapdoors. This very practical form of construction has been used on a number of different canals, and appears again with a variation on a later warehouse on the Trent & Mersey at Rode Heath. Though the basic idea is the same, the main walls of the building fall sheer to the water, and the arch merely supports a separate loading tower or locum, rising above the main canal.

Shardlow can be thought of as a canal new town, a child of the Georgian age – even if many of the genuine Georgian buildings have gone to make way for pseudo-Georgian replacements. We may think of it as being old fashioned in a rather dignified way, but in its time it was a place that believed in making use of all the latest technology. Cast iron was an important cargo for the canal boats, but also found its way into local structures. Those semi-circular windows appear as standard off-the-shelf fittings in the nineteenth century catalogue of the Andrew Handyside Foundry in Derby. Another Derby firm, the Phoenix Foundry, provided castings for milestones for the local turnpike roads, and cast iron milestones were also made for the canal. A survivor at Shardlow informs boaters that they are now ninety-two miles from Preston Brook. This versatile material extended beyond the purely practical. As the town grew with the increased prosperity brought by the canal and the industries it attracted, from boat building to rope making, so the citizens felt they needed a

*Cast iron appears regularly along the canal in the form of mile posts in a very distinctive style that can also be seen on the surrounding roads.*

church of their own. St James, built by public subscription, looks suitably grand, but the tracery of the Perpendicular style windows is not traditional stone, but cast iron, no doubt delivered by canal.

The growth of the new towns of Shardlow and Preston Brook is a testament to the importance of this new transport system. A far more important effect of the canal, however, can be seen in the growth of manufacturing centres, such as the brewing town of Burton-on-Trent and the Potteries. Burton had been a brewing centre for many centuries, but with the coming of the canal there was now a means of transporting the beer by water to Hull for export, not just to the rest of Britain but to Europe as well. Barges could travel, using the wide locks of the Trent & Mersey on to the Trent, generally trans-shipping to coastal vessels at Gainsborough on the tidal river. Among those who saw the possibilities offered by improved transport was a small-time carrier who ran a brewing business as a sideline, William Bass. With the opening of the canal in 1777, he abandoned carrying to concentrate on his brewing. He contracted with another carrier, Matthew Pickford, who was beginning to build a fleet of boats. Both concerns were to become hugely successful: Bass remains a major brewer, while Pickford's went on to become one of the most important carriers on the whole canal system, before moving on with the times, first to the railways, then back where they had begun, on the road. Not much of this can

*This small roundhouse once stood at one end of Josiah Wedgwood's great Etruria pottery. As one of the principal promoters of the Trent & Mersey, he ensured that his new works had a canal frontage and he kept a personal eye on traffic from his home, Etruria Hall, which still stands.*

be read directly from the buildings beside the canal which, although they show a linear development along the waterway, are generally Victorian or later and reflect the parallel route of the Midland Railway, opened in 1839. Some idea of the former importance of the canal can, however, be gauged by the extensive Horninglow Wharf area and the derelict Shobnall Basin, poking a watery finger into the heart of the town. It is certainly true to say that in the early years, companies such as Bass depended heavily on canal transport, and with the extension of waterway links down to London, the company ended up owning its own warehouse complex at Paddington Basin.

The effect on the Potteries is perhaps more apparent in the development of canalside works, a few of which still retain their distinctive bottle ovens, though none of these remain in use. The most important of all the works that deliberately located beside the canal was the Wedgwood factory at Etruria, a name which arose from a mistaken belief by Wedgwood that his pottery was based on Etruscan ware. Almost nothing of this once immense factory survives, but the house Wedgwood built for himself, Etruria Hall, a somewhat glumly classical building, still looks down over the canal. If there is little to suggest what a mighty enterprise this once was, there are at least reminders of one of the most important cargoes brought to the works. Powdered flint was used to whiten the earthenware pottery, and the raw material was brought round the coast from East Anglia to Hull to continue its journey by river and canal. At Etruria, by the top lock of the Stoke flight, is the former Etruscan Bone and Flint Mill, a substantial works with its own basin, which used steam power for the work of grinding. This is an evocative site, not just because of the flint mill. The locks bring the canal to the summit level, and a maintenance yard and toll-house were established here. Its great appeal, however, lies with the canal structures themselves, the contrasts in colour, texture and form; cobbled paths snake round curved brick walls at the lock side, the mellow red of the brick throws into relief the spiky iron of winding gear and the angular black and white of balance beams. It is also the starting point for a branch canal, the Caldon, completed in 1779. Here is a canal that attracts modern boaters for the delights of its scenery, but which has an important industrial history that can still be read in the buildings and structures met along the way.

The wording of the original parliamentary act is interesting for it introduced a whole new idea into the canal world. It allowed for a canal from the Trent & Mersey to Frog Hall 'and a Railway from thence to or near Caldon… and to make other Railways'. Caldon was Cauldon Low, a limestone hill which was extensively quarried. There was no way that the canal could be expected to climb a hill that rose about 600ft above what was to become the village of Froghall, hence the need for railways. The man behind the quarry enterprise was John Gilbert, who designed a waggonway with wooden rails, which was completed in 1778. It is ironic that it should have been Gilbert who made the first rail connection to a canal, by laying down what we would now call a tramway. This was a form of transport which his employer, the Duke of Bridgewater regarded with deep distrust, famously prophesying that the railways would eventually prove a dangerous rival to his beloved canals. The first system was not a success, and major changes were made in 1783. The canal itself was extended

*Flint was a vital ingredient for the potteries and this grinding mill, now a museum, stands near the top of the Stoke flight of locks. While it can be seen to have a long wharf and its own basin, road access is actually quite poor, emphasizing the value of canal bulk transport.*

over a quarter of a mile to reach its present terminus at Froghall Wharf, which involved digging a seventy-six yard long tunnel, and the wooden track was replaced by cast iron rails set on timber baulks. This too was to have a short life, largely because the concern was so successful. In 1804, John Rennie arrived on the scene and constructed a double-track plateway, on which the rails were set on square stone sleeper blocks, leaving a space down the centre for the horses that would pull the trucks. There were four self-acting inclines, up and down which the trucks were hauled by cable, the weight of the full trucks heading down to the wharf being used to pull up the empties. Gravity did the work, hence the name 'self-acting' and progress was controlled by brake drums at the tops of the slopes.

There were to be further changes through the years, but this remained the basic system by which the quarries were linked to the canal. Most of the limestone was initially burned for fertiliser. Lime kilns were built at the wharf, seven of them by 1795, together with a small brick kiln. Froghall was a scene of immense activity, and stone crushers were later added to the kilns. Today, all that has ended, but the wharf area remains, the old plateways can still be followed as footpaths and the remains of the kilns can still be seen.

It requires an effort of imagination to recreate the idea of life at Froghall at its busiest, but another important site on the canal is almost perfectly preserved, and beautifully illustrates the way in which an industrial site could be integrated with the transport system that served it. For much of its length, the Caldon canal follows the

Although the Caldon Canal is, in effect, a branch of the Trent & Mersey its character is very different as these two photographs from Stockton Brook show. The lock is the standard design, but the bridge across the tail is very new. It consists of two platforms cantilevered out on iron brackets with a gap in between to allow a tow rope to pass straight through. Nearby, instead of the familiar bridge of stone or brick, is this lift bridge with its overhead balance beams.

line of the River Churnet – and at Oak Meadow Ford lock the canal actually enters the river, leaving it a mile further on near Consall Forge, once the site of a small iron works. But the river has another role to play in the story, for its waters were used to provide power for Cheddleton Flint Mill. The site was chosen for two reasons: there was already a corn mill on the site which could be adapted for its new role, and it was close to the canal. Two waterwheels drive the grinding machinery, but what is of interest here is the way in which the whole site has been laid out on the basis of the canal bringing in the raw material. Before flints can be crushed they have to be calcined, heated in a kiln to make them brittle. As the canal at this point is a good deal higher than the river, the builders have been able to construct the kilns into the buttressed bank below the wharf. As a result, when a boat arrived the flints could be unloaded and shovelled straight into the open top of a kiln. Then, when the heating process was complete, the calcined flints were loaded into small trucks and carried away along a short plateway to the mills. The site was developed at the same time as the canal was being constructed, and shows that time and motion studies were not an invention of the twentieth century.

These are only two of the many sites of interest along the Caldon; there were more flint mills at Consall and limekilns at Cheddleton and Horsebridge. Among the other interesting features of the canal are the bridges, a mixture of

*A busy scene at Hazelhurst locks. It is difficult to imagine now, but these locks were once abandoned and derelict and only restored to working order in the 1970s.*

conventional brick bridges on the pattern established on the Trent & Mersey and lifting bridges. There is also one oddity, Cherry Eye Bridge, which for no obvious reason was built with a Gothic, pointed arch. Such architectural embellishments were generally down to the whim of some local landowner, wishing to beautify the view from his house or grounds. On the whole, it was easier for the canal company to give in, rather than engage in a lengthy dispute over land purchase. In this case, it may well have been the owner of the extensive woodland that borders the river valley who wanted a note of grace in the landscape.

The most imposing of all the structures seen along the seventeen-and-a-half mile long canal belongs to the last phase of development. An act of parliament of 1797 allowed for an extra branch from what is now Hazelhurst Junction to Leek and also had provision for a reservoir to feed the canal system. The Leek branch begins by running alongside the Caldon, where the latter drops down through the Hazelhurst locks. The Leek branch stays on the level, then swings round to cross the older canal on a handsome, single arched aqueduct. It is a structure of considerable grace, and clearly belongs to a later generation, when canal engineers had grown in confidence. The reservoir to the north west of Leek is long, thin and enjoys an attractive setting. As Rudyard Lake it is something of a local beauty spot, its origins in the mundane task of topping up canals largely forgotten. Among those who enjoyed boating on its waters were a Mr and Mrs Kipling, who liked it so much they gave its name to their son. But we have moved ahead of the main story, and it is time to go back to the 1770s, James Brindley and the earlier canals.

*Water supply is vital to any canal but because reservoirs are often some distance from the canals they serve, they are easily forgotten. Rudyard Lake now looks quite natural but was actually created in the 1790s.*

# 4. The Cross

Even before work had begun on the Trent & Mersey, plans were being laid to extend the system to link in the other two great navigable rivers of England, the Severn and the Thames by other new canals, which together would form what became known as The Cross. The first to come to fruition, with a parliamentary act of 1766, was the Staffordshire & Worcestershire, which was to leave the Trent & Mersey for a cross country route to the Severn. This was soon followed in 1768 by the act for the Coventry Canal, which would link that city to the Trent & Mersey, and which would also be linked to the third new canal, the Oxford, begun in 1769, which in turn would complete the line down to the Thames. There was one other vital component to the scheme, a canal which was to generate a vast amount of traffic for the system as a whole, and make its proprietors wealthy men; the Birmingham Canal, linking the rapidly growing industrial town of Birmingham, via Wolverhampton, to the Staffs & Worcester. The story of the early Birmingham developments will be dealt with in the next chapter, and in this section we shall concentrate simply on the scheme that was eventually to link all four rivers to form The Cross.

In many ways, the most interesting of these canals is the Staffs & Worcester, for it most clearly shows both the virtues and shortcomings of its chief engineer, James Brindley. As on the Trent & Mersey, he followed his preferred method of hugging the river valleys for as long as possible, going to considerable lengths, literally and figuratively, to avoid obstacles rather than tackle them head on through heavy engineering works. So, as it leaves the Trent & Mersey at Great Haywood, the canal initially heads west, closely following the line of the River Sow, before turning due south along the valley of the Penk. Brindley had few changes of level to worry him, just two locks in the journey beside the Sow, but he did have to construct two aqueducts, crossing first the Trent then the Sow. The alternative he could have selected can be clearly seen by looking at the way in which railway engineers tackled the same terrain when they came to build their line running to the south of the canal, the Trent Valley, opened in 1847. Had Brindley followed a similar course, he would have needed just the one river crossing, but he would have also required a tunnel and a deep cutting or second tunnel. It is easy to see why an extra aqueduct was the more appealing option.

His first ever aqueduct at Barton had been the wonder of the age, but these were far more modest. Looking at the Sow aqueduct, the first obvious point is that it is not crossing a navigable river, so there was no need to build high arches to allow boats to pass underneath. The approach, however, seems to lack the boldness shown earlier

*The aqueduct carrying the Staffs & Worcester over the River Sow. It is, in canal terms, surprisingly inelegant, with blunt, stubby piers and harsh angles to the parapet. It looks much clumsier than the Barton aqueduct (see page 28).*

on the Bridgewater. The Sow is a far more modest river, but the aqueduct is carried on four segmented arches, lined with brick. The masonry consists of bulky, squared, but irregular stone blocks, with a prominent string-course and a parapet. It is sturdy and functional, but could never be called graceful. Much the same can be said of the Trent aqueduct. The aqueducts are like almost everything else one meets on this stretch of the canal, designed to minimize complications. The exception can be seen at Tixall Wide, where the canal suddenly broadens out. This was not Brindley's choice, but an example of a canal company showing itself anxious to please a powerful local landowner. The owner of Tixall House, Thomas Clifford, called in the well-known landscape gardener, Capability Brown, to improve his grounds.

*The splendidly extravagant Tixall gatehouse looks out to the canal, which has been broadened at this point to turn it into a passable imitation of an ornamental lake in keeping with the grandeur of the scene.*

Brown was famously fond of lakes in his gardens, but rather less keen on commercial waterways. The answer was a compromise, where the canal as it passed the house was widened into a fair imitation of an ornamental lake. The house has now gone, but the wonderfully elaborate sixteenth century gatehouse still looks out over the water. One could say that canal promoters themselves should carry part of the blame for the extra work. Thomas Bentley, Josiah Wedgwood's one time partner, wrote a pioneering pamphlet, setting out the case for canal construction, and, in an attempt to woo the wealthy, rhapsodized over the delights of having 'a lawn terminated by water'. The Cliffords of Tixall got just that.

The canal continues on its way, hopping from river system to river system, keeping as close as possible to the natural contours, until it finally arrives at the River Stour, which is followed all the way to the Severn. A story that has been much repeated over the years has Brindley going to the prosperous river port of Bewdley with the idea of creating the river junction there, only to be rebuffed by the local worthies and rudely told to take his 'stinking ditch' elsewhere. This is, in fact, just the opposite of what really happened, for Bewdley actually petitioned to have the canal come to the town, as they would have welcomed the extra trade. It would have made sense in many ways, for Bewdley was already well supplied with facilities – warehouses, stabling for some 400 pack animals and such useful industries as rope making. Unfortunately, a ridge separated the river from Kidderminster, the nearest point from which the canal could have been turned away from the Stour

*The baroque magnificence of Tixall gatehouse stands in marked contrast to nearby Tixall lock, with its simple cottage and plain brick bridge, its lines emphasized by the paintwork.*

towards Bewdley – and crossing ridges did not fit the Brindley ideal. He opted instead for the far easier route, continuing down the Stour to a point on the Severn, graced by a single inn, and here the junction with the river was made. It gave birth to the town of Stourport.

Stourport is the most impressive of the inland ports to grow up out of early canal developments. This is not surprising, for the Severn was one of the busiest rivers in Britain, and barges of all kinds regularly traded up to and beyond the new junction. The canal itself ended just north of the mouth of the Stour, at a height of 29ft above the Severn. It was decided to build a canal basin at this level to keep it clear of flooding, an ever present danger on the Severn, which has not lessened with the years. In the first stage of development, there was a single basin, connected to the river by broad barge locks, able to take vessels up to 75ft long with a 15ft beam, so that the basin itself became the trans-shipment point, and a toll-house was built to collect the revenue.

The canal, however, soon proved a huge success, so a big expansion programme was put in hand in 1781. A new basin was built immediately to the west of the original, and two more were added at an intermediate level, between these and the river. All were interconnected and now, as well as the two barge locks, there were four narrow locks for canal boats, built as 'risers', in which the top gates of the lower lock are also the bottom gates of the one above. This contrasts with Brindley's ideas on lock building elsewhere on this canal, as we shall see shortly, but it is an efficient system. At the heart of this complex stands the splendid Clock Warehouse, a two-storey brick building, which was given its handsome clock tower and weather vane in 1812.

The town grew rapidly with the increase in trade. Houses and shops were built in the area surrounding the basins, and had all the charm that one would expect of a Georgian town. The stylishness even extended to the commercial buildings: there is a particularly good example just above the first lock up from the basin, a warehouse built out over two arched loading bays, and enhanced by attractive cast iron tracery in the windows. Development continued at a good pace round the basins, and the original toll-house was demolished, and a new one built further up the canal in 1853. As well as the people who lived and worked in Stourport on a

*The wide barge locks leading up to the basin at Stourport, which is dominated by the large warehouse with its ornate clock tower.*

*The narrow lock that joins the Staffs & Worcester to the Severn at Stourport. The bridge carrying the river towpath across the canal is pleasingly complex, with its wing arms curving beside the steps. The old wooden bollard sculpted by years of use stands behind its modern replacements.*

*During the extension of the canal basins at Stourport, the original toll-house was demolished and a new one built further up the canal. For a small building it is quite elaborate, with its prominent bargeboards and finials, reflecting Victorian not Georgian taste.*

permanent basis, there was also a growing number of visiting traders and merchants needing accommodation. Local speculators got together to build the Tontine Hotel, which got its name from the curious system used to finance it. In a tontine, when one investor dies, his shares are parcelled out among the survivors, a process which continues until just one is left as sole owner. One can only imagine the keen interest shown by the families in the health of their elderly relatives as the numbers dwindled. It was built in a very grand style, with a hundred rooms, all offering comfortable accommodation. Its importance can be gauged from its elaborate façade, enlivened by a central bay where the main entrance is flanked by large windows, their arches heavily emphasized by prominent keystones. The river boatmen had to make do with the far more modest Angel on the bank of the Severn. The commercial success led to the creation of two more basins by the river, the Furthermost and the Engine, but the arrival of the railway and the building of the new river bridge, moved the axis of development westward, leaving Georgian Stourport as an almost self-contained entity.

The actual work of canal construction began at Compton on the edge of Wolverhampton, at the southern end of the summit level, in the summer of

*Georgian Stourport grew up around the canal basins and spread down to the river bank. The town grew and developed further, and the power station downstream served the later industries.*

1766. By then, the fateful decision had been taken on the width of Harecastle tunnel, and it was here that Brindley built his very first narrow lock, together with a wharf and a substantial bridge to carry the main road over the canal, so that it remains a site of considerable historic interest. From here, the canal follows the line of the Smestow Brook south to The Bratch, where it takes a sudden plunge downhill. This is perhaps the most extraordinary feature to be found on any Brindley canal. Here three locks drop the canal by 30ft, and at first glance they appear to be interconnected to form a staircase, an enlarged version of the risers built later on at Stourport. But not a bit of it – each lock is separated from the next by a very short pound, considerably less than a boat's length. This means that there is nowhere to go with a boat until the next lock is ready, a very inconvenient arrangement, as boats cannot pass each other along the flight. It is also slightly baffling, as there seems to be nowhere for the water to go as the upper locks empty. In fact, side ponds have been terraced into the hillside, to act as mini-reservoirs. In practice, the flight has to be worked like a staircase, which just happens to have more gates to open and more paddles to wind than are really necessary. It is difficult to see what made Brindley decide to opt for such a clumsy arrangement, and it was certainly not something he repeated anywhere else. But that does not mean that The Bratch looks inelegant: it is in fact one of the most attractive group of locks to be found on any canal, and all the appeal comes from a mixture of simple responses to functional requirements, with just a suggestion of embellishment for its own sake. A bridge crosses the tail of the top lock, and its parapet with rounded coping swings round in a smooth curve to form a wall between the road and the lower lock. So tight is the bend, that a recess is let into the abutment to allow for the swing of the balance beam. At the opposite end of the bridge is a toll-house. Where the Stourport toll-house has the charm of a bay-fronted cottage, this is more like a belvedere or gazebo in some fine gentleman's park, a delicious octagonal building, with a symmetrical array of round headed windows and a neat conical roof. This is architecture, not vernacular building, a rare phenomenon in the canal world.

Below The Bratch, the convolutions begin to set in as the canal worms its way round increasingly dramatic sandstone outcrops, and not always succeeding even then. At Cookley, a short tunnel had to be driven through the rock, not in itself a great problem as the stone is easily worked and strong enough to be self-supporting. The presence of the attractive orange-red stone adds greatly to the appeal of the canal, but the very character that makes it easy to tunnel through also makes it generally unsuitable as a building material. It can, however, with a little ingenuity be used to advantage as at Debdale Lock, where cave-like stables have been carved into the cliff. The sandstone not only sets the visual mood, but it dominated the way in which the line was set out, forcing Brindley to adopt ever more extravagant curves, with the canal at times doubling right back on itself. To those who come this way by boat or by walking the towpath, it is often difficult to see where the canal might be going next as yet another sandstone cliff rears up,

*Brindley had to set his canal line wherever he could at the western end. Here at Falling Sands, it hugs the tall sandstone cliffs that literally overshadow the narrow lock.*

seemingly blocking the way. The battle to find a way through for the canal is seen at its most dramatic at Austcliff where it squeezes under a great overhang, dripping with trailing plants and ferns.

The tortuous progress ends only at Kidderminster. This is one of the few big towns on the route, famous as a carpet-making centre, which like the industrial towns on the Trent & Mersey found growing prosperity with the arrival of improved transport. Here, at least, there are still ample signs of a continuing industrial life, but elsewhere important complexes have vanished and their canal connections have died with them. At Pratt's Wharf, an area of rather sad neglect, there are the remains of a lock that once gave access to the neighbouring River Stour. This short branch served the old Wilden Forge, which had been taking pig iron from the Forest of Dean, by way of the Severn, since the seventeenth century. In the early years, the iron was unloaded at Redstone Rock, a mile south of Stourport, but now it could be brought all the way to the works by water. At the forge, the iron was worked using water power, and now virtually all that remains is Wilden Pool, with its system of sluices and channels to feed the water wheels. If nothing else, it serves as a useful reminder that this canal, now travelled almost exclusively by pleasure boats, was once a vital part of a thriving industrial world.

*Modern pleasure boaters see the Staffs & Worcester as an idyllic rural waterway but it was built to serve industry. Here at Kidderminster nineteenth-century carpet factories line the canal. An unusual feature is Brinton's Mill chimney in the background with a pattern of blue and yellow bricks and false lancet windows. Sadly the mill was demolished in 2001.*

Returning now to the northern end: above Compton lock, the canal enters its summit level, swinging round the outskirts of Wolverhampton to Aldersley where there is a junction with the Birmingham Canal – the next junction at Autherley is of a much later date. Beyond this point, the canal enters one of its rare straight sections. Brindley would have preferred to take a more roundabout route, as he was faced with rock very close to the surface and lying directly in his path. But any detour would have been far too long even for him to contemplate. Reluctantly, he set his men to hack and blast a channel; but with no machinery to help in the work it must have been desperately hard going. To minimize the labour, he took the same decision that he had at Harecastle, cutting a channel just wide enough to allow a single boat to pass through at one time: good news for the navvies, bad news for boatmen facing an irritating bottleneck. Having taken a straight line once, he was not disposed to keep to it and soon reverted to type, swinging his way round hill and valley. There were, in any case, practical advantages in having a long summit, since it could also act as a reservoir. It was not sufficient in itself, and three small reservoirs were built near Gailey, and the now abandoned Hatherton Branch also acted as a feeder. But one can see the price that had to be paid to keep on the level, in the great U-bend that was made simply in order to minimize the engineering works needed to cross a tributary of the Penk. Brindley's

*Gailey was an important place, where the Staffs & Worcester was crossed by Watling Street, the modern A5. Here, as well as an extensive wharf is the first of the locks taking the canal down from the summit. Such a key site was marked by the unusual castellated round house.*

decisions often seem almost arbitrary: As we shall see later (p.65), he was quite capable of taking a more direct line, earthworks and all.

The summit ends at Gailey lock. A little way above this is Gailey Wharf, with another architectural curiosity. Where the toll collector was given an octagonal house for all round vision at The Bratch, here he got it quite literally, with a round tower instead. This does seem to be a canal where the unusual has become the norm. Locks are usually supplied with some means for taking excess water round a lock instead of allowing it to flood straight over the top, generally in the form of stepped overspill weirs. Brindley chose instead to build circular weirs leading down to culverts, rather like giant plugholes.

There is one other very notable structure on this northern section of the Staffs & Worcester, the junction bridge at Great Haywood. Here the towpath of the Trent & Mersey is carried over the arch, that of the Staffs & Worcester under it. To make the way easy for the horses crossing the bridge it has been given long approach ramps and a wide, shallow arch. It is a fascinating exercise in the geometry of curves, with the parapet rising to a point above the segmented arch, and the widening wings of the approach ramp are also built on a pronounced curve. It is rightly regarded as an outstanding example of both the designer's and the builder's craft.

The Staffs & Worcester proved a very successful canal and is perhaps the best example of Brindley's work, for it was completed in his lifetime, on time, and, remarkably for any civil engineering work of the period, almost within budget. Looking through the canal records one often finds a long list of acts following on after the first, in each of which the proprietors were applying to parliament for permission to raise more capital. The Staffs & Worcester is a

*An obvious requirement for the canal is a system for allowing excess water to flow round a lock when it is not in use. Brindley provided the Staffs & Worcester with circular weirs, the outflow kept clear by a 'lobster pot' cage.*

notable exception. They only returned once, and that was after completion, to get permission to improve the Severn between Stourport and Worcester. It was the river authorities who were not keeping pace with the demand created by the busy canal. The same story cannot be told of the next canal, the Oxford. Begun under an act of 1769, it was not opened throughout until 1790, so it does not have the same sense of being the work of just one guiding hand. There were problems from the start.

The stated aim was to form a link with the Coventry Canal, and so make a connection to the rest of the Midland system, but no one could agree where the junction was to be made, each company hoping to extend the length of its own waterway in order to maximize the income from tolls. So, for a time, the farcical situation existed where the two canals ran side by side. Then, far more seriously, the money ran out and work proceeded on a stop-start basis, with various

*Haywood Junction bridge is greatly admired as an example of the builder's art. The visual excitement comes from the flow of lines and the balance of shapes, creating an organic, sinuous structure out of something that is essentially functional.*

engineers being called in. After Brindley's death in 1772, work passed to his assistant and brother-in-law, Samuel Simcock.

Following the line laid down by his old master, Simcock completed the line north from Banbury, eventually reaching an agreed junction with the Coventry in 1777. There for a time things halted, until parliament approved the raising of extra funds. In 1779, Robert Whitworth joined Simcock in surveying the line south from Banbury. In the event, Whitworth's views prevailed, but it was not until 1787 that the Company could raise the investment to finish the canal. The end result was a canal that shows different characteristics for its different building phases. Even then, the opening of the canal did not mark the end of major changes, for in 1828 Marc Isambard Brunel was invited to re-survey the northern end of the canal to provide a better link through to Birmingham. The result was that the old wandering line went and what was in effect a new straight canal was constructed striking through the meanders of the original line and lopping 14 miles off the journey. The northern Oxford, in its present form, will be dealt with in a later volume.

The one section of the canal that remains unmistakably Brindley's, lies between Banbury and Braunston. It follows the pattern we have already seen, climbing out of one river valley to reach a long, serpentine summit, before dropping back down to the next valley. Not everything is quite as it was, having been shifted sideways at one point with the arrival of the M40. Essentially, however, the route remains much as it was when built, once one is clear of Banbury. A lock in that town was hit by a bomb in 1942, but the damage done was as nothing compared with the havoc wreaked by post-war planners. Very little of the old survived, but astonishingly there was one exception, the ramshackle collection of buildings where the Tooley family built and repaired wooden narrow boats. It achieved fame in canal circles as the place where L.T.C. Rolt acquired his narrow boat *Cressy*, and here it was refurbished, with the traditional paintwork finished by old Mr Tooley in person. It is perhaps the last reminder that Banbury has that the canal was once the town's most important transport route, a large part of the extensive wharf area having been razed to the ground to make way for a bus station.

Heading off north, the canal at first follows the line of the modest River Cherwell through a scatter of locks. It passes villages of immense charm such as Cropredy, which it might seem, pays very little attention to the canal on its doorstep. Yet this was a bustling place when the canal was new. Records show that in the 1790s over 2000 tons of coal a year were unloaded at the village wharf. There was a toll-house here as well, and the canal was deliberately narrowed down to a single boat width so that vessels could be gauged. The canal official had a calibrated gauging rod, and by measuring the height of a side above the waterline he could calculate the weight of cargo on board and the tolls to be paid. The final climb to the summit is through the Claydon locks, grouped together as a flight of five, and raising the canal by over thirty feet. The village itself sits well back from the canal, but this is still an interesting spot. The top lock before the summit was a good place to site a maintenance yard, particularly with a village close by. It is a very simple affair of rich, mellow brick with smithy, workshops and stabling. The main buildings form an L, enclosing two sides of the wharf, with an open colonnade for easy access and storage, and there were once extensive stables on the far side of the lock. The yard is no longer operative, converted to other uses back in the 1970s, but the charm has never been lost and, as so often on this canal, it derives in large measure from the materials, local brick and tiles, used with a total absence of pretension.

The area above Claydon is farmland, undulating and seemingly unchanged for centuries. But there have been changes, still recorded in the landscape. Medieval fields were turned to pasture by the improving farmers of the late seventeenth and eighteenth centuries, their old pattern of ridge and furrow still preserved as giant corrugated sheets of green. The canal builders showed no interest in old field patterns and cut their way across boundaries, so that one of the features that occurs quite often on the Oxford Canal is a wave-like border where ridge and furrow have been sliced open. The steady rise and fall of the landscape and the dotting of tree covered knolls make for a picturesque scene, but not one to gladden the heart of a canal engineer. One can still imagine James Brindley plodding along on his aged grey mare, eyeing the undulations with a jaundiced eye, working out how to thread his canal through the maze of hillocks. Inevitably, he threw his canal into startling bends and twists, culminating in a quite extraordinary section at Wormleighton Hill, which the canal almost circles. Those who travel the canal pass the front door of the house on the hill, note that it is an elegant building and think no more about it until, about twenty minutes later they find themselves back again, this time at the back door. It seems an extreme case of contour cutting, simply to avoid quite minor obstacles, but engineers never had total freedom. The local bigwigs of Wormleighton Manor were not over keen on having a canal at all, and were particularly firm about allowing no locks, which they said would give boatmen an excuse to stop, hop over the fence and acquire a pheasant for the pot. They were more than happy for the new canal to be tucked away round the back of the hill.

*Faced by Napton Hill with its windmill as a prominent landmark, Brindley took the Oxford Canal down through a long flight of locks, and then swung sharply away to skirt the foot of the slope in a sweeping curve.*

63

In among the squirms and wriggles comes one ruler straight section, heading off down a deep cutting to the wharf at Fenny Compton. It does not look in the least like anything else on any other Brindley canal. In fact, it was originally a tunnel bored through the low hill, which at 1,138 yards long was one of the biggest engineering works on the whole canal. It was, like the other Brindley tunnels, narrow, but broadening out to passing places and fitted with a series of iron rings which boatmen used to haul themselves and their vessels through. It was an inconvenience, and in 1838 the company was able to acquire all the land above the tunnel. The two ends were opened out, together with a portion in the middle, leaving just two short underground sections. By 1870, the whole tunnel had been opened, creating the long, deep cutting we see today.

The advantage of a long summit for water conservation has already been mentioned, but here the process was taken a stage further. The channel was dug eighteen inches deeper than usual, which it was estimated would be enough to supply an extra four locks a day. It was still not sufficient for the large numbers of boats expected to be using the canal, so extra supplies had to be created by building reservoirs. The first was built at Byfield Water near Boddington and the second at Clattercote, north of Banbury. It is easy to ignore reservoirs, yet they play a vital part in the running of the canal and rank among the more important civil engineering features of any canal. The feeder from Clattercote runs for two miles with a fall of 36ft, and for 869 yards of the way it runs in a tunnel. A good deal of surveying skill and careful construction was needed to maintain a steady gradient over such a distance, particularly when so much is underground. A third reservoir was later added at Wormleighton, with a feeder which crossed the line of the canal above Fenny Compton tunnel. When the tunnel was cut open, an aqueduct of riveted wrought iron plates on brick piers had to be built to carry the water over the cutting.

The canal's eleven-mile summit ends at Marston Doles. From here a flight of nine locks leads the way down, rounding the flank of Napton Hill. The village itself perches high above the canal with a tower windmill as a prominent landmark. From having followed its often wayward track heading north, the canal is now forced round on a more easterly route. What appears to be a branch canal at Marston Doles, below the first two locks of the flight, represents part of another solution to the problem of water supply. A steam-pumping engine was installed in the 1790s to lift water from below ground and discharge it into a brick-lined channel. The boiler house could be supplied with fuel by water along what became known as the Engine Arm, a short navigable feeder with just one bridge along the way.

At Napton Junction, the whole nature of the canal begins to change. The next section, between Napton and Braunston, was eventually to become a part of the important Grand Union system, providing a more direct line between Birmingham and London than that offered by the Thames and southern Oxford. It still remains, however, an essentially rural canal, a particularly good stretch in which to look out for medieval ridge and furrow, but the canal structures seen along the way mainly belong to the later period of development.

*1. The Bridgewater Canal emerging from the mine at Worsley Delph, stained by ore from the workings.*

*2. Warehouses converted into flats at one of the early canal settlements, Preston Brook where the Bridgewater meets the Trent & Mersey.*

3. The two Harecastle tunnels on the Trent & Mersey: Telford's on the left, Brindley's with its low, narrow opening on the right.

4. A lock at Fradley on the Trent & Mersey, with the black and white of the balance beam contrasting with the curves and rich brickwork of the bridge.

5. A misty morning on the Trent & Mersey by the old brewery at Stone.

6. Wood, stone and iron create intriguing patterns at Middlewich. (Trent & Mersey).

*7. Hazelhurst Junction with the Caldon Canal leading down through the locks and the Leek Arm turning away to the right, soon to cross on an aqueduct.*

*8. The elegant toll-house stands above the locks at The Bratch on the Staffs & Worcester.*

*9. A rare straight line on a Brindley canal. This started as the Fenny Compton tunnel on the Oxford Canal but was later opened out.*

*10. The old office by the gate providing road access to Coventry basin.*

*11. Practical but attractive – Hartshill maintenance yard on the Coventry Canal.*

*12. Hawkesbury Junction where the Oxford and Coventry canals meet. The engine house in the background once held a Newcomen pumping engine.*

*13. The little used Spon Lane locks on the old line of the Birmingham Canal.*

*14. The steam narrow boat* President *passing under the railway viaduct while ascending the Wolverhampton locks.*

*15. The Stourbridge Canal heading down towards the Redhouse glass cone.*

*16. The Birmingham & Fazeley towpath curves gently over one of the many arms that once led to wharves and basins.*

*17. The Farmer's Bridge locks on the Birmingham & Fazeley, overwhelmed by the modern city.*

*18. Part of the old canal world that has survived on the Digbeth branch of the Birmingham & Fazeley.*

*19. Salt's Mill with its Italianate chimney stands beside the Leeds & Liverpool at Saltaire.*

20. *The Leeds & Liverpool in the heart of the Pennines at Farnhill.*

21. *The unusual double-arched bridge at East Marton.*

*22. One of Britain's most attractive flights of locks at Greenberfield. The water supply control building stands next to the lock cottage. (Leeds & Liverpool).*

*23. Cast iron columns and brackets carry a warehouse canopy over Eanam Wharf in Blackburn. (Leeds & Liverpool).*

*24. A bye weir cascades down from a lock on the Rufford branch of the Leeds & Liverpool.*

*25. Unusual gear on the Rufford branch: the handle is turned horizontally to raise the ground paddle by means of a screw. (Leeds & Liverpool).*

26. The former Pickford's warehouse arching over the Chesterfield Canal at Worksop.

27. The extraordinary lift bridge on the Huddersfield Broad Canal with its massive counterweights.

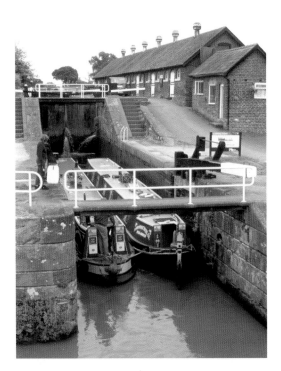

*28. A pair of hotel boats, motor on the left, butty on the right, entering Bunbury locks on the Chester Canal.*

*29. Sandiacre lock on the Erewash Canal epitomizes all that is best in canal architecture.*

*One of the major engineering features on the old canal was the tunnel at Newbold-on-Avon. The western portal has been blocked in up to water level. Originally the roof arch was continued as an invert, giving an oval cross section (A. Burton).*

This is especially true after Braunston, where the new shortened canal begins, but even so it is an interesting area to explore to find out what remains of the original line. When the route was straightened, the old meandering curves were not simply abandoned, for they still served a purpose as branches off the main line to small village wharves. In time, however, they proved uneconomic and gradually fell into disuse. Perhaps the most rewarding section for exploration is to be found near Newbold-on-Avon. The modernized canal heads resolutely towards its junction with the Coventry, passing through a short tunnel. Down by the church, however, is the original tunnel of 1777, with the shallow trough of the dried out canal running at right angles to the newer line. The tunnel itself is an oddity, for it was begun in a rather grand manner, with a five-foot wide towpath and a high arched roof. There was concern, however, that excavations on such a scale were likely to undermine the church, so at about 100ft into the tunnel it was shrunk to allow for just a three-foot towpath and the profile was changed to a lower arch. Following the line away from the tunnel mouth, brings one to old brick bridges, standing alone and crumbling among the fields and a wharf area serving no visible community. It is not difficult to see why the loops were eventually abandoned.

The most imposing feature of the canal was also one of Brindley's boldest engineering works. At Brinklow, the canal had to cross over the valley of the Smite Brook. This time there was to be no great detour. Instead he designed an

*The meanders of Brindley's original Oxford Canal north of Braunston were preserved for a time as branch lines. Today, the occasional bridge can still be found standing over a stagnant, reed-choked ditch.*

aqueduct, carried on twelve brick and stone arches, each with a 22ft span, with embankments at either end, so that the whole complex stretched for a quarter of a mile. It would have seemed simpler to have made the whole crossing on a bank, culverting the stream and piercing the bank where necessary for access. Brindley, however, seems to have decided that he had been quite daring enough already, and he was nervous of such extensive earthworks. He made a virtue of necessity by designing the arches as usable spaces, as a stable, a fodder store, a blacksmith's forge and even designating some of the arches to be used as dwellings. The latter might seem a bizarre notion, but it was not uncommon in the eighteenth century for similar archways under tramway embankments to be occupied, and the rattle of iron wheels on iron rails overhead must have been a good deal less comfortable than the quiet swish of a canal boat. The arches have mostly been filled in, but the bank remains an impressive feature, and one can still glimpse the excellent work done by Brindley's masons in the neatly squared stones at the river crossing.

After this rather startling departure from what we think of as the usual Brindley pattern of construction, he reverted to type, and the canal was sent off again on as devious a route as that at Wormleighton. It can still be traced, wriggling off under the M6 to the south of the present line, round Nettle Hill, then winding up north again towards Hopsford. It is no wonder it was said that in the early years of the canal a boatman could travel all day within the sound of Brinklow's church clock striking the hours. For the final mile, the Oxford ran close by the Coventry, from

*Although modernization brought many changes to the Northern Oxford, there are survivors from the past. Here a working boat turns off under the mellow, red-brick bridge for the basin at Hillmorton maintenance yard.*

Hawkesbury down to Longford. Eventually the meeting point was agreed, but there was a problem. The two canals were supposed to have been built at the same level, but as the Oxford was actually six inches higher, a shallow lock had to be constructed. For a time, this was a busy place with a wharf and toll office, but the absurdity of having two canals running side by side for a mile eventually became obvious to even the most obdurate officials.

The situation was rationalized, and a new junction created at Hawkesbury, and the last mile of the old Oxford was filled in. All that remains now is a row of cottages in Hollybush Lane, which were originally built alongside the canal. The new junction at Hawkesbury, known to generation of boating families as Sutton Stop, developed a character all its own, while replicating some of the old features of Longford, the toll-house and shallow stop lock. It became one of those places where the constantly moving families from the boats could meet, stock up on supplies, exchange gossip and, very important to the younger family members, chat up the opposite sex.

The centre for all this activity was the then unpretentiously plain Greyhound Inn, which doubled as a general-purpose store. This was an area dominated by the canal, with wharves and offices, cottages and cobbled lanes. Inevitably, much has changed, but a good deal of the old atmosphere remains. What has gone forever is the working environment, the collieries that supplied a major part of the cargo for the boats. They may not, strictly speaking, have been a part of the canal world itself, but they gave it context and meaning. A solitary reminder is the engine house near the junction. A Newcomen engine, the earliest practical form of steam powered beam engine was installed to pump water from nearby Griff Colliery. It was later moved to the present site, where it continued to remove water from the local mines, but also fed the drainage water directly into the canal system. The engine was eventually replaced in the 1830s by a more modern steam engine, but the original has been preserved as a working memorial to its designer Thomas Newcomen, in his home town of Dartmouth.

The final section of the canal to be completed, the line from Banbury to Oxford itself and on to the Thames, presented the engineers with few problems as it remains in the Cherwell valley throughout most of its length. It is a section full of delights, the valley dotted with almost ridiculously attractive villages, many built in the local lias stone, tinged and bronzed to a golden, toasty brown by the presence of iron ore. It is a building material to match the more famous Cotswold stone, and often turns up in bridges and warehouses where the canal cuts through the stone belts. In fact, this canal provides a perfect example of how builders settled for local materials wherever possible, and one can see how structures correspond to the underlying geology, ranging from Oxford clays to oolitic limestone. At Somerton Deep lock, the cottage is brick, but a wonderfully rich-

*The lock cottage at Somerton Deep Lock sits at the heart of the typical rolling agricultural land of the Southern Oxford. The cottage itself is a little unusual in having a vaguely Gothic air with pointed arches above the windows.*

*The lift bridge is very much a feature of the canal between Banbury and Oxford. It requires the minimum of construction works. The canal is pinched in by stone walls and the platform simply drops down to close the gap.*

coloured brick. The building itself seems quite plain at first glance, but has unexpected detailing. Windows are square, but set back into round headed recesses. Little arched windows in the gable ends provide look outs along the canal. The bridge over the tail of the canal is also built of the same brick. Further south, it is no surprise to find that the bridge by the Rock of Gibraltar pub is of stone, from the nearby quarry. As it originally carried the main road, it is a dignified, low arched structure with sweeping lines, a marked contrast to its modern, squared off featureless replacement. But all this construction work was being undertaken by a canal company with a serious cash shortage, so wherever possible, the cheaper option was taken of building lift bridges to meet the needs of farmers and landowners. These were even cheaper to build than swing bridges, consisting simply of a wooden platform with hand rails, pivoted at one end, with the other end sitting in a stone-lined recess on the opposite bank. The platform was raised by pulling down on bulky balance beams, set at an angle; the whole structure was not unlike a lock gate turned through ninety degrees. In all there were originally thirty-eight of these lift bridges and forty-one more substantial road and wagon bridges, twenty-one built in stone and the rest in brick.

Although for much of its length this remains an essentially rural section of canal, it was of great importance to the villages along the route, each of which had its wharf, even if wharf buildings were not always supplied. Sometimes, as at Shipton-on-Cherwell it may now appear as nothing more than a flattened area of ground beside the bridge, overlooked by the church. Elsewhere, as at Lower Heyford, wharf and wharf-warehousing survive, adapted for a new commercial use as home to a boat hire base.

*The bye weir or overspill weir at Northbrook Lock. Here excess water collects in a small side pond then falls over the weir to a culvert. Note how the company saved money by using single gates at both ends of the lock.*

One settlement stands out as particularly interesting, the hamlet of Thrupp. There were houses and farms here before the canal came along, and one set of cottages was bought to form the basis for a maintenance yard. They still have the character of farm cottages, built in the local vernacular with stone walls and thatched roofs. The presence of a maintenance yard, a wharf, local villages, and an important paper mill by the greatly diminished settlement of Hampton Gay, made this a busy little spot that grew with the arrival of the canal. A row of cottages was built facing the canal that still stand, but a second group has gone round in a circle - converted into a Baptist Chapel in the nineteenth century and turned back into housing in the twentieth. The Boat Inn has also known changes, starting off as The Axe, then becoming The Unicorn before achieving its present name, which at least accurately reflects its main function for many years, assuaging the not inconsiderable thirsts of the boating population.

In its course down the Cherwell valley the canal has no lock flights, just a steady scattering of single locks, twenty-eight of them, spread out along the 27 $\frac{1}{2}$ m route, but not everything is quite as straightforward as it might appear. At Upper Heyford, the canal was being built just to the east of the river, but the way ahead was blocked by rising ground. There were two obvious options: cut through the hillside or cross the river on a low aqueduct. The engineers opted

*Near Aynho, river and canal converge. The next lock, Aynho Weir Lock is built as an irregular octagon to make sure sufficient water is passed on to the canal between here and Oxford.*

for neither. They decided to move the river instead, diverting it into a new artificial channel. An old mill that had stood on the east bank of the Cherwell in its old course was demolished, and a new mill constructed, that can now be seen on the west bank of the river. For a small community that had scarcely seen any change in centuries, this bizarre hopping of mills across rivers must have seemed quite extraordinary. Near Shipton, the river begins to turn away in a more easterly direction, no longer following the line towards Oxford. This time, the canal would have to change sides, and it was to do so by joining the river for about a mile, then parting again at Shipton Weir Lock. The difference in level is only 2ft 5in and the only water passing down to the lower level of the canal is that which passes through the lock, the rest continuing to flow off down the river. This shallow lockful would not have been enough to fill the deeper locks further down the canal, so a special lock was built here, octagonal in shape, making up in surface area what it lacked in depth.

Interest heightens as the canal nears Oxford. The Duke of Marlborough was owner of extensive paper mills at Wolvercote, where the canal was due to pass close by the river and at a very similar level. He negotiated the right to make a short cut between the two, with one lock, which would allow for the inevitably varying levels of the river. The Duke's Cut, as it is still known, thus provided the first direct access to the Thames for boats travelling down from the Midlands. But the canal proprietors were well aware that there was an immense demand for coal in the city and the canal was continued south, with numerous small wharves along

*The closeness of river and canal and the slight difference of levels is very clearly seen between Shipton and Enslow, where the two run side by side. The canal is at the slightly higher level on the right.*

*The first junction between the Oxford Canal and the Thames is made via the Duke's Cut, which leads away past the junction house making a tight turn under the bridge.*

the way, passing under Hythe Bridge and Worcester Street to reach an extensive coal wharf built in the shadow of the old castle. This part of the canal was later sold off, filled in and Nuffield College now stands on the site of the former terminus. But one building, at least, has survived, and it gives an indication of the grandeur of the canal company in its heyday. The former head office was built by the wharf in a typical neoclassical style, with pilasters embellishing the side walls and a prominent portico at the front. Above the portico is the company emblem carved in stone, showing Britannia holding a shield adorned with the Oxford coat of arms, while behind her, with a touch of artistic licence, the canal can be seen sweeping past the Radciffe Camera, a building which it never came near. It is now rather a forlorn sight, tucked away down an alleyway, a reminder of past glories.

Today, the canal comes to an abrupt end at Hythe Bridge, and just above that is Isis Lock, leading to the second cut to the Thames. It was constructed from the old Sheepwash Channel, which was dredged and made navigable by the Thames Commissioners. Then, at long last, the canal system was complete, for the basin could not only be used by narrow boats, but could also be reached by barges trading along the Thames. Oxford became a trans-shipment point, just as Shardlow and Stourport had done some years before. Furthermore, with the completion of the Coventry Canal, the Oxford was to become part of a genuine, national waterway system.

*The final approach to Oxford through Isis lock, which has a delightful bridge which, being cast iron, definitely does not date from the early period of construction. Below the lock is the Sheepwash Channel down to the Thames.*

The Coventry would seem to offer the fewest problems of any of the canals of The Cross. It was planned to be thirty-eight miles long with just thirteen locks, eleven of them grouped into the Atherstone flight, and just two more from there to the junction with the Trent & Mersey at Fradley. There was one river crossing, over the Tame, by a typical aqueduct of stone and brick carried on three arches. The one short tunnel en route has long since been opened out. There were no major engineering problems to delay construction, but the company soon found itself deep in trouble. The arguments with the Oxford over the junction have already been mentioned, but the Company felt, rightly or wrongly, that their engineer could not work for two rival concerns and actually had the temerity to sack the great man. Even that would not necessarily have created too many difficulties, if the company had not run out of money. By the end of 1771 the canal had reached Atherstone and there it stuck, the money all spent and no one prepared to invest the extra capital to carry it through to a conclusion. Work restarted in the 1780s, but only because help was available from two other sources. The Birmingham & Fazeley Canal Co. (see p.95) had obtained an Act that allowed them to construct a canal from the Birmingham to join the Coventry at Fazeley. They would then continue on, heading for a meeting at Whittington Brook, where they were to be joined by the Trent & Mersey Canal Co. building the other half of the new canal, and starting in the north, to complete the through route to Fradley. So, with a little help, the original line was finished, but was now divided

*A statue of James Brindley has been given pride of place in the recently refurbished Coventry Basin.*

up between three separate companies. In time, the Coventry was able to buy out the Trent & Mersey interest, leaving them in the odd position of owning a dismembered canal. They had twenty-seven miles from Coventry to Fazeley, then there was a gap, followed by the final seven miles of what became known in the official books as the 'Detached Portion'. However, it is more convenient to consider it as just one canal, as was originally intended.

The terminus at Coventry consists of a wide basin, with cobbled yard and a peninsula to increase the length of wharf. The present warehouse buildings only date back to the 1830s, and show the influence of later developments in docks such as Telford's complex at St Katharine's in London. The roof is carried out over the wharf on supporting pillars to create a canopy for loading and unloading in the dry, with hoist covers set into the roof like gargantuan dormer windows. Weather boarded hoists, brick walls and slate roofs make for a very pleasing contrast. New development has all but enclosed the basin, leaving a small circular brick office, which once stood at the road entrance to the wharf, and now stands in elderly isolation. The new developers have at least acknowledged the man who began it all, with a statue of James Brindley inspecting his plans.

The journey from Coventry to Hawkesbury is something of a pilgrimage through the city's industrial history; it shows that, even in the nineteenth century, a canalside site was still considered valuable, particularly for factories and works that needed cheap coal for their steam engines. The service by boat from colliery to factory wharf was still the cheapest system available. The best known of the early canalside buildings were built in 1857 by Joseph Cash, a local entrepreneur and philanthropist. He lived in an age when craftsmen were being forced out of their homes and into factories. He recognized that the handloom weavers were unable to compete with the new power looms, but he could at least do something to preserve the old way of life where the weaver went direct from his living area up to the workshop on the upper floor of his house. Cash's solution was a whole row of terraced houses, not with individual workshops, but with one continuous loomshop running the whole length of the row, filled with power looms, driven by belt and shaft from a central steam engine. At the start of day, the workers simply went upstairs to emerge through trapdoors. The firm prospered and built up a near monopoly in producing name-tapes, which went to identify the school clothes of generations of children. All this developed from the cottage industry of ribbon weaving, and one can still see the old weavers' cottages with their distinctive, large windows further along the canal.

Industries of all kinds jostled to find the best site, among them the nineteenth century Coventry Cotton Factory, which was later to become the site on which two new companies developed, both begun by Henry Lawson – the long

*Cash's Top Shops lining the canal near Coventry. The two lower storeys with their small gardens seem to represent a conventional Victorian terrace. What makes this building different is the continuous workshop, with its large windows, running above the houses for the full length of the row.*

*The Coventry Canal formed a vital link between collieries and the surrounding towns and industries. The pits have closed, but an indication of the scale of activities can be seen in the immense heaps of spoil overlooking the canal.*

forgotten Great Horseless Carriage Co. and the considerably more successful Daimler Motor Car Co. It is ironic that the motor industry of Coventry, which was to play a leading part in killing off commercial carrying by narrow boats should have begun in a building specifically designed to take advantage of precisely that older form of transport.

The Coventry Canal rarely strays far from its industrial origins. Although the mines that fed it are now closed, the spoil heaps remain, grassed over perhaps, but still unmistakably man-made hillocks in the landscape. Modern developments crowd around much of the canal, but it still has its very own, particular delights to offer. There are few spots that better demonstrate the general rule of all early canal buildings, that a concern for function allied to a simple use of appropriate materials can result in buildings as attractive as many deliberately designed by architects with the aim of pleasing the eye as the main requirement, than Hartshill maintenance yard. The buildings are neat and workmanlike, but individual features are gracefully executed; round-headed windows are matched by blind arches that decorate the walls – all echoing the practicality of having a wide arched opening to allow boats to pass inside, for this is the feature that sets the visual pattern. Curves are what one notices here. The main building stands back from the canal, approached by a short arm running away at an angle, so walls are rounded to minimize any damage that might be caused by boats making the sharp turn. The importance of the building is emphasized by an ornate clock tower, but even that also serves a practical function through its ventilation louvres. It is a gracious building, but the clutter of cranes and hoists serve as a reminder that it was built first and foremost as a working yard. The immediate area also provides clear evidence of the importance of coal mining to the region – and to the prosperity of the canal, with immense spoil heaps rising above the waterway.

The plans for The Cross were drawn up in an atmosphere of high optimism at the beginning of the canal age, but the scheme took far longer to reach a conclusion than even the most pessimistic expert could have foreseen. It was neither the fault of the engineers, nor of the promoters who employed them. If anyone should carry the blame, then it would be the politicians who led Britain into a disastrous war with America, which resulted in the whole country diving into a deep, financial depression. Other canal schemes, however, were going forward at the same time in various areas, and rather more speedily than the Oxford and the Coventry. None were more successful than those centred on Birmingham.

# 5. Birmingham

One thinks of Birmingham as a vast conurbation, a modern city that extends with no apparent break until it rubs shoulders with its newly-aggrandised neighbouring city of Wolverhampton. It is difficult to imagine what the area might have been like in the middle of the eighteenth century, but it is necessary to have some idea in order to understand the manner in which the canal was built, what effect the canal had and just why it was to prove so important. Samuel Bradford made a map of Birmingham in 1750 showing it scarcely larger than a village, surrounded by a scatter of hamlets. What the map cannot show is just how busy this little town had become, a place of small workshops, turning out everything from fancy buckles and buttons to sacks of nails. A quarter of a century later another cartographer, Thomas Hanson, produced his map of Birmingham, and by then it had grown quite dramatically. What had happened in between was the construction of the Birmingham Canal. It is all made quite clear when the two maps are compared, for the area that had been developed lay between the new wharf at the canal terminal and the former town boundaries. A road had been built, appropriately named Navigation Street, along which were rows of new houses and commercial properties. It was boom time in Birmingham, and the canal lay at the heart of it.

Like any developing industrial centre of any era, one of the keys to success is an efficient transport system, and in the eighteenth century that meant canals. Unfortunately for Birmingham it stands on a plateau, which the other early canals had avoided. The Coventry skirted it to the east, the Trent & Mersey to the north and the Staffs & Worcester to the west, so if the citizens and manufacturers of Birmingham wanted canal access, then they would have to provide it for themselves. They raised the money, and did what almost every other promoter of that time had done: they called in James Brindley. He was to set out a line from the outskirts of Birmingham, across the plateau to Wolverhampton. Although the two towns were almost at the same level, an inconvenient ridge lay between them. After that, there was no option but to plunge down to the Staffs & Worcester at Aldersley. The parliamentary act was passed in 1768 and the account of the canal given in John Phillips' *History of Inland Navigation* of 1801 gives a notion of the sort of terrain through which it was to pass. From Birmingham it 'proceeds to Wilsden-green and Smethwick, by Blue-gates, West Bromwich, Oldbury, over Puppy-green, by Church-Lane, Tipton, and Bilston, by the skirts of the town of Wolverhampton, by Gosbrook-mill, near Aldersley, into the Staffordshire canal.'

This makes it sound like a line that was to link small villages and settlements, rather than one to be constructed through a built up area, and that is just what it was. And that meant that Brindley had a great deal of freedom to set his canal out through what was then largely open countryside, with none of the restrictions that would inevitably have been imposed by having to negotiate his way through crowded towns. What he settled for was a typically long route. As with the northern Oxford, we can make direct comparisons, for this was such an important canal that it was bound to be updated as the new technology became available. This time it was to be Thomas Telford who designed the new main line, carving through the central ridge in deep cuttings, as a result of which the twenty-two mile long journey by the Brindley canal was reduced to just fifteen miles. This time, however, most of the old canal has survived, simply because so many important industries had been developed along its banks, and they still valued and needed canal transport. So what had once been immense, sweeping bends were retained as loops off the new line – Oozells Street Loop, Icknield Port Loop, Soho Loop and so on. As a result the Brindley canal survives much as it was built, with just a few modifications in the form of improvements or adaptations where it crossed the new line and its branches.

As one would expect, Brindley kept his canal on the level as far as was possible, but he still had that inconvenient ridge to deal with, so he climbed up to it at Smethwick through six locks and then after a very short summit of little more than a mile, dropped back down again through another six locks to reach the Wolverhampton level. After that came the sharp descent through a twenty-lock flight to Aldersley. There were also two important branches to Ocker Hill and Wednesbury to reach the all-important collieries. These branches were considered so vital to the whole enterprise that they were constructed long before the main line was completed down to Aldersley. Many of the Birmingham proprietors would have been happy to stop at that, for they now had the cheap coal they so desperately needed, and it required a certain amount of pressure from the Staffs & Worcester to persuade them to fulfil their legal obligations.

It is now extremely difficult to get more than a vague overall impression of how the original canal might have looked as so much has been changed, swept away altogether or obliterated by later developments. The old loops do still exist, even if they are seldom used, but travelling along them is an utterly different experience from what it would have been when they were first constructed, with later buildings crowding in along what were once rural sections. Even the canal itself has been subject to considerable changes: the locks at either end of the summit have been reduced to two sets of three. This was always a problematical area for water supply, which was partly solved in 1778-9 when Boulton & Watt steam pumping engines were installed at each end of the summit, so that the water that came down the locks could be pumped back up again. Brindley or one of his assistants created another and quite unnecessary water problem at the very end of the line. The bottom lock of the Wolverhampton flight was originally ten feet deep, around twice the depth of the other locks, so there was a real difficulty in supplying sufficient water to refill it.

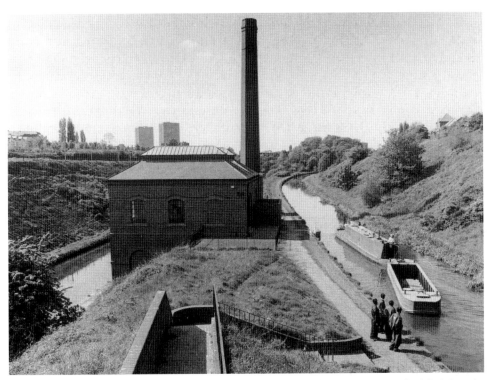

*Two generations of Birmingham Canal building on view at Brasshouse Lane. On the left, below the pumping house, Telford's new canal heads off through a deep cutting, while the old Brindley line goes wandering round the hill.*

This problem was solved by replacing the single deep lock by two conventionally sized locks, creating the modern flight of the Wolverhampton 21.

The overall problem of water supply was tackled by the provision of reservoirs at Tipton and Smethwick – the outlet for the latter, Rotton Park reservoir, being a prominent feature on the Icknield Port Loop. Another valuable source was, once again, water pumped out of mines. The distinguished engineer John Smeaton who was brought in to advise on the whole question of water supply in the 1780s calculated that the canal as a whole needed to be supplied with 965 lock-fulls a week of which 478 came from mine drainage. But, however helpful mines might have been in that respect, the benefits were offset by the effects of subsidence, which in some places had caused the bottom of the canal to drop by as much as a foot. It was the constant struggle to provide water, as much as anything else, that led the company to pay for improvements, first by Smeaton, then by Telford. The result can be seen most clearly at the summit, where there are three distinct levels, Brindley's original, Smeaton's level below that and the modern main line built by Telford, slicing through it all in deep cuttings.

The first terminus of the canal at the Birmingham end was at a large basin, where the canal divided to pass round two sides of an open wharf. It was overlooked by handsome offices, built with an unusual octagonal block in the centre, opposite the end of Paradise Street. The offices were demolished in the 1920s and television studios now occupy the site of the filled-in basin. The canal was later extended to Cambrian Wharf, which was always meant to be the end of the line according to the original Brindley design. This was to become one of the first examples of an old basin being given a modern restoration to create an urban amenity. The treatment was very sympathetic. Old buildings, including a little row of eighteenth century cottages, were refurbished, hand cranes were retained on the cobbled wharf and a new canalside pub, The Longboat, built. The latter may not be very distinguished, but it has the great virtue that it is very much orientated towards the canal, with canal boat themes inside. For years the canals had been regarded as unpleasant, smelly ditches whose main value to the local community was as a dumping ground for anything from unwanted prams to dead dogs. From this time canal enthusiasts were no longer alone in finding them attractive: many discovered the pleasure of standing out on the balcony, enjoying the play of light on the water, with the scene enlivened by the occasional passing boat – even the occasional working boat. It was from this modest beginning that Birmingham woke up to the realization that the canal system was an asset rather than a liability. The Cambrian Wharf scheme received a well-deserved Civic Trust award in 1970.

From the wharf the old canal begins to wobble away, like an old soak at closing time, round the short Oozells Street Loop, then turning through the

*Looking more like a seaside picture, this is Rotton Park Reservoir, dried up in the summer of 1995. It plays a vital role in water supply for the Birmingham Canal.*

*The Telford canal heads ruler-straight for its objective, while the old wriggle on the Brindley canal has been reduced to the Soho Loop, emerging from under the little bridge on the left.*

giant U-bend of Icknield Port Loop, hemmed in by mainly nineteenth century industrial buildings, rising sheer from the edge of the canal. Returning to the new main line, it cuts straight across it, this time swinging round the even longer Soho Loop, named after the Soho Works of the most famous of all Birmingham manufacturers, Matthew Boulton. He was already a prominent figure when the canal was promoted but his fame was to spread throughout Britain and beyond when he formed a partnership with James Watt and they began building steam engines at Soho. These works were extended in the 1790s and a new foundry opened, reached by a short arm off the canal, just to the west of the loop. Little now remains of the original factory.

Everywhere along the length of the Birmingham Canal one finds evidence of change and adaptation, particularly noticeable where the old canal meets newer

*The style of lock and bridge at Smethwick is typical of the Brindley age, and the presence of industrial buildings crowding in on the canal explains why the old route was kept open after the new main line was completed.*

arrivals on the scene. A new aqueduct had to be built to carry the Brindley canal over Telford's at Spon Lane. There are more changes a little further along, for the old junction with the Wednesbury Arm has gone. The arm no longer has a direct connection with the old canal, but has a new starting point at the Telford line, and has also been extended far beyond its initial modest $3\frac{1}{2}$ miles to form the Walsall Canal, with extensive connections to other parts of the system. Another late aqueduct crosses the Netherton Tunnel branch, the second of the Dudley Canals. After that the old line went off on its most extravagant meander, now forming the Wednesbury Oak Loop, which unlike the others has been partly filled in. That it has survived at all is simply because at the far end are the maintenance yard and workshops at Bradley – plain, neat buildings with no architectural pretensions, standing beside a good sized basin. Being a dead end, this part of the old system gets even less use than the other loops, so that coming this way by boat is, to say the least, challenging.

Change is very much the order of the day around Wolverhampton. Close by the junction with the later Wyrley and Essington Canal, begun in 1792, is the district known as Horseley Fields, where iron works existed for two centuries and where the development of the industry was closely liked with the growth of the canal system. The area at the top of the locks thus took on particular importance; it was close to a major industrial complex, it gave easy access to Wolverhampton itself, and to the rest of the rapidly growing network of the Birmingham Canal Navigations (BCN), where one could find a variety of

*The Malthouse Stables stand by one of the bends on the old canal at Tipton Green, but were actually built with stalls for fourteen canal boat horses as late as 1845.*

boats. There was quite enough trade on short runs between collieries and factories to keep fleets of day boats busy. The simplest were straight-sided, with almost vertical stem and stern posts, and in some cases were double-ended, so that the rudder could be hung at either end. This had the great advantage that there was no need to wait until a winding hole was reached, a specially broadened section of canal in which a boat could turn, before setting off in the opposite direction. Towing mast and helm were simply moved, so that what had been the bows on the way out became the stern on the way back. The most basic vessels were simply open boats, but others known as 'Joeys', had a small cabin. Alongside these were boats intended for longer journeys to other parts of the expanding canal system. All were allowed for along this stretch. Canalside works often had their own arms for easy loading, and the

*The Birmingham Canal leaves the plateau, which has provided a comparatively easy passage, by charging downhill through the Wolverhampton 21. The top lock has a typical terrace of small, very urban cottages, somewhat altered over the years but with the characteristic materials of brick and slate.*

*By the bottom of the Wolverhampton flight, the city has been left behind and the surroundings are wholly rural. Here one finds the familiar contrast of stone against brick, emphasized by the ridges on the lock-side ramp that provide sure footing for horses.*

former Minerva Works in Minerva Lane actually had two, mainly used by day boats. The long-range haulier, Pickford's, had their wharf close by, with basins where their boats could be tied up while waiting for cargoes. Even the arrival of the railway, which parallels the Telford line for much of its length, did not simply take trade away.

The wharf of the former Chillington Iron Works was adapted for use as a covered canal-rail interchange, with railway sidings built along the edge of the wharf. After this bustle of activity, the twenty-one Wolverhampton locks take boats down the hill and off to the country. It all ends where an old brick bridge, slightly unusual in having a straight parapet instead of the familiar curve, crosses the tail of the bottom lock. Beyond that is the quiet junction with the Staffs & Worcester, which the Birmingham reached in 1772, just six days before Brindley died. Already by this time, plans were being drawn up for extensions to the system.

The first connection was made by what was then known as Lord Ward's Canal, after its promoter the resoundingly named John, Second Lord Viscount Dudley and Ward. He was the owner of extensive mines at Castle Hill, Dudley, which yielded limestone, coal and fireclay, all valuable commodities that were used in local ironworks. The Birmingham Canal already ran close to the site, and in 1775 work began on the new canal, which was just under half a mile long. This might make it seem to be of little interest, but 226 yards consisted of a tunnel through to the mines of Castle Hill. This was only the start of what was to become one of

*A trip boat heading into the northern end of Dudley Tunnel. The entrance at the foot of the limestone cliff looks small, but the gauging bar hanging from the roof indicates that some parts are even lower.*

the most extraordinary achievements of the canal age, the creation of a watery labyrinth with over three miles of tunnels. The first extension of the original system began in 1776, when work started from the far side of the Dudley hill to join another new canal, the Stourbridge.

By 1784, the big decision had been taken to link the two segments of what was now the Dudley Canal by extending the tunnel. The work was to go on right through to 1792, when the main line of the Dudley Tunnel was opened up to complete a second link from the Birmingham Canal down to the Staffs & Worcester at Stourton Junction. More links were to follow over the years, as the BCN grew and developed, and the old Dudley tunnel carried less and less traffic until it was officially closed in 1962. But thanks to the efforts of volunteers, the through route, including the 3,154 yards of navigable tunnel, was reopened in 1973. Because it was built in the days before boats had engines, there was no allowance for ventilation to remove exhaust fumes, which could build up to dangerous levels in the often very narrow bore. It remains closed to motorized vessels, but special trips are available in electrically powered boats along what is certainly the most remarkable canal tunnel in Britain. It has been altered and modified through the years, but with its mixture of different bores, lined and unlined sections and the different rock strata through which it passes, it repays careful consideration. In it one can see the different problems faced by the engineers and the different solutions they found, during a period that covered nearly a quarter of a century of work.

Approaching the tunnel from the north, the Birmingham Canal end, the first section to be reached is the original Lord Ward tunnel which is brick-lined and unusual in having a shallow arch for the roof, instead of the semi-circular arch found on the Brindley canals. Along the tunnel, in the lined sections, there is evidence of construction techniques in the gaps in the brickwork, into which scaffolding was fitted. These were often left as 'weep holes', allowing water to escape from behind the brickwork. Many of these holes have calciferous deposits hanging like frozen drapery down the wall. The first section opens out at Shirt's Mill Basin, with wharves for loading the material brought from side-tunnels that ran off on both sides of the basin to reach the limestone mines. After this brief visit to the open air, a second short length of lined tunnel is joined, which emerges under a great rock arch to reach Castle Mill Basin. This was the end of the first tunnel and was originally a vast, roofed cave, but has long since been opened out to the sky. Three tunnels meet here, including the branch to more extensive limestone workings at Wren's Nest Hill.

The main tunnel at the far side of the basin is the start of the extension, on which work began in January 1786. At first it is unlined, passing through an area where the strata of Wenlock shale can be seen running at an angle of 45° to the horizontal. This is a brief interlude before the tunnel opens out into one of the most remarkable of the man-made features, the Cathedral Arch. One can see how it got its name, for this underground junction is covered by a vault, rising over thirty feet above the water. Once again, this is a point where a complex system of

*The southern end of Dudley Tunnel hints at a later date than its northern counterpart, with its brick portal, stone voussoirs and parapet, and pilasters picked out in blue engineering brick.*

*The Black Country Museum. The arm of the Dudley canal is crossed by an iron bridge brought here from Wolverhampton, and beyond that is the basin with its immense lime kilns.*

now closed tunnels led away to yet more mines and quarries. For the remainder of the journey, lined sections alternate with exposed rock – shales, limestone and two types of sandstone are all visible. It is still possible to see the smooth semi-circular grooves, which represent the surviving halves of holes bored through the rock and packed with powder for blasting. Construction shafts have been capped but are still prominent features, dripping with water and lined with two centuries of mineral deposits. The oldest lined sections have rough, reddish bricks made at or close to the site, but more modern, hard, blue engineering bricks also put in an appearance. In places the tunnel narrows down and the roof seems so low that there hardly seems to be enough space for a boat to pass. It all ends at the southern portal at Parkhead, reconstructed almost a century after work first began, having been rebuilt in 1884 out of Staffordshire blue bricks.

It might be thought that nothing else on the canal could match the drama of the tunnel, but happily this is not quite the case. Even the short arm from the Birmingham Canal at the Tipton end is packed with interest. A large basin was constructed here and an extensive range of limestone kilns built above the wharf in the 1840s. This area is now part of the Black Country Museum, with displays showing many different aspects of the local canal scene. The short canal arm to the basin below the kilns is crossed by an ornate cast iron bridge that originally carried the road across the canal in Wolverhampton. Threatened with demolition, it was dismantled and re-erected here. From Parkhead to the junction with the Stourbridge is just over two miles, but in that distance the canal has to make its descent from the Birmingham plateau. There is a gentle beginning through quite open landscape, with the remains of a disused branch to Netherton and the first modest group of three locks, soon followed by a junction with the Dudley No.2 Canal. This was built to relieve pressure on the original, always a sign of success – far better to have too many boats than too few. Another reminder of later changes and the need to increase water supply to the growing system is the pumphouse by the Parkhead locks. This was all difficult, undulating country for the engineers to deal with, and after the canal has dropped down the isolated lock at Blower's Green, it gives a couple of wriggles before arriving at the top of a steep slope and the locks still known to many as the Dudley Nine, even though the flight was completely rebuilt with just eight locks in the 1850s.

Not so long ago, this was an almost aggressively industrial scene, dominated by brick and fireclay works, foundries and collieries towards which the canal dashed downhill. Now the industrial past has been swept away, factories have been replaced by houses and in the process the lock flight has also been given

*The Dudley Nine or Delph locks heading down for a junction with the Stourbridge Canal. The former stable block can be seen on the left, while what appears to be a stream on the right is the cascade created by the bye weirs.*

a face-lift. It remains exceedingly impressive, the locks closely packed together, with single gates on the uphill side and double on the downhill and just enough space in between for balance beams to swing without fouling. The overspill weirs run into side ponds to conserve water, and these in turn are linked to form a cascade running parallel to the locks. The locks themselves are of considerable interest, with sharply pointed piers at the tails of the locks, reminiscent of the cutwaters of river bridge arches. Although stone is used for the lock chambers, coping for walls uses the hard, blue bricks of the region. There is a reminder, too, that this was a vital part of the whole Birmingham system, for the paddle gear supports still have the initials BCN cast into the ironwork. A small stable block can be seen at the top of the flight that now houses a small museum. At the bottom the canal makes an end-on junction with the Stourbridge.

The canal passes under the modern road bridge, but the towpath is still ridged to help the boat horses that once came this way to maintain their grip on the slope. In spite of the changes brought about in recent years, there are still reminders of the industrial days, with the towpath carried over bridges that once crossed side arms and basins, now filled in and in the first section built over with new housing. The canal takes a wayward line past the spoil heaps from old mine workings, eventually reaching a T-junction. To the north are the remains of the Fens Branch, which serves as a feeder from the Pensnett reservoirs, while to the south the main line continues down a flight of sixteen

*The lock cottage halfway down the Stourbridge flight is unusually grand. It stands above a double lock, with a split cast iron bridge crossing the tail of the upper lock.*

locks, which are in many ways similar to the Delph locks in their use of materials and in having extensive side ponds, though some of these have been enlarged to create basins and wharves. Here one finds the use of a material that was, in later years, to become one of the favoured structural materials of the BCN – cast iron. A constant problem for bridge builders, where there was a change of towpath – in this case to gain access to wharves – was what to do with the towrope, which had to go under the arch even though the horse was going over the top. The early builders solved that by making long approach ramps, each descending on the same side of the bridge. Here the new material allowed for a more elegant solution. The bridges are usually described as split

*Stourbridge town wharf is dominated by the restored bonded warehouse. Seen here from the road, the most obvious feature is the curved wall. Waggons heading for the yard on the right had to make a sharp turn and any that hit the wall would slide off instead of causing damage.*

*Dwarfed by the large buildings that now dominate the canals in the centre of Birmingham, the little toll house at Farmer's Bridge marks the junction between the Birmingham and Birmingham & Fazeley Canals, and here boats paused to pay their tolls as they moved from one canal to the other.*

bridges, but in effect what one has is two sets of iron brackets supporting platforms that do not quite meet in the middle. Now the towrope can simply slide through the gap.

Half way down the flight is the 'double lock' and next to it an unusual lock cottage. It is an L-shaped, three-storey building, with a two-storey extension that was used as an office. It has been altered over the years, the original arched windows having been squared off. Nearing the bottom of the flight, the view is dominated by the hundred-foot high glass cone, built around 1790 for the Redhouse Glassworks, and now belonging to Stuart Crystal. It is superficially similar to the bottle kilns of the potteries, and like them it works as a giant chimney for a central furnace. Here, however, men actually worked inside the cone, drawing the molten glass from the fire and working it in side chambers. At the time of writing, the wharf area by the canal was being restored. Close by the cone is the canal complex of Wordsley Dock, with a basin overlooked by a timber-built warehouse with a broad canopy, traditionally known as 'Dadford's Shed'. A row of brick cottages and a pub complete the scene.

*The Ashted locks lie on a branch for the Birmingham & Fazeley which originally ended at Digbeth basin, but now links into the later Grand Union system. Modern developers have appreciated that the canal can be attractive and not just a dumping ground for supermarket trolleys.*

At the foot of the locks the way divides. The Town Arm turns away towards the centre of Stourbridge, passing other modern glassworks along the way. It ends at the town wharf and the grand Bonded Warehouse, built in 1799 and extended in the 1840s. A feature of the construction is the rounded corner by the road which, as with the warehouse referred to at Shardlow (see p.40), allowed wagons to negotiate a difficult turn without causing damage to the building. The main line, meanwhile, continues on its way, crossing a short aqueduct over the Stour for a brief rural interlude before arriving at the village of Stourton. A last flight of four locks leads down past a small lock cottage and a basin to reach Stourton Junction. Here the towpath of the Stourbridge is led up the long approach ramp of a brick bridge, to join a new towpath on the far side of the Staffs & Worcester.

The final link for the first generation of canals centred on Birmingham was forged in 1783, with the passing of the act for the Birmingham & Fazeley, linking

*Aston Junction shows many of the features typical of the Birmingham canal scene. The cast iron bridge fabricated at Horseley Ironworks was built as part of the extensive developments of the nineteenth century. Along the canal a bridge rises in a low arch carrying the towpath over the entrance to an old basin.*

the Birmingham with the Trent & Mersey and the Coventry. Although this was primarily conceived as a junction canal, it also had an important branch serving the busy industrial centre of Digbeth. The original act also gave a hint of things to come when it allowed for the amalgamation of the new company with the Birmingham to form what became known as 'The Company of Proprietors of the Birmingham and Birmingham and Fazeley Canal Navigations', which within ten years was shortened to the Birmingham Canal Navigations, the familiar BCN.

Few canals have been quite so overwhelmed by modern developments as the Birmingham & Fazeley. There is a brief reminder of the past in the neat little toll office, with its projecting bay giving a good view of both canals, which meet here at Farmer's Bridge Junction. This is not a memory of a rural past, but simply records the fact that a bridge had to be supplied when the canal was first built across Mr. Farmer's land. The little office competes for attention with a wealth of new buildings, including the National Indoor Arena. The good news is that in the immense building programme that has transformed this area, the developers have treated the canal as an amenity to be cherished, not as an oily backwater to be hidden away from view. From here, the canal drops down through a flight of thirteen locks with a total fall of eighty feet. They are packed close together and plunge through an artificial canyon of buildings that not only crowd both sides of the waterway, but one building has even been built right over a lock, encasing it in concrete pillars. Bridges cross arms leading to nowhere, the industries they served

*The old and the new: the Birmingham & Fazeley overwhelmed by the concrete pillars of the motorway interchange best known as Spaghetti Junction.*

having closed and their successors having no interest in water transport. The overtaking of the canal world by later developments is emphasized by the railway that strides over the canal on a high viaduct and even more dramatically by the sudden eruption of noisy traffic on the Aston Expressway near the foot of the locks.

At the Expressway, the canal swings through a right-angled turn, where the Digbeth Branch leads off down the six Ashted locks, with one interruption to the journey at the short Curdworth tunnel. A good deal of restoration work has been done with excellent results. Bricks have been relaid on the lock surrounds, with brick ridges set into the ramps at the access bridges. The use of blue engineering bricks for edges and copings provides a pleasing contrast with the rusty colours of the paving. The branch, like the main line, presents a mixture of the old and new, with the elaborate ironwork of the Victorian gasworks reflected in the bronzed glass of a modern office block. The old creeps in again at Belmont Row, where a canal house even has space for a small garden. Back at the main line, the route continues north down through the eight Aston locks and three more isolated locks to reach Salford Junction. This was not part of the original route, but was created with the arrival of two later canals, the Tame Valley and the Birmingham & Warwick Junction. It is nowhere near as complex, however, as the roads that meet overhead, the famous Gravelly Hill Interchange, better known as Spaghetti Junction. These roads are carried on immense concrete supports that appear all round, alongside and even in the canals.

The Birmingham & Fazeley now follows a very obvious line, down the Tame valley, but with little change in the immediate surroundings. Erdington Hall bridge may seem to offer hopes of old style grandeur, but all that materializes is what seems to be a short tunnel, roofed in concrete, actually the underside of one of the industrial buildings that continue to dominate the route. Grandest of these, but now looking rather forlorn is Fort Dunlop. One factory, the Cincinnati Works has been kinder to its neighbour than the rest, with landscaped gardens leading down to the water's edge. Minworth locks mark the real change in the landscape; the Tame valley spreads out and industry recedes, while the canal retains a comparatively straight course, falling steadily through a scatter of locks. The generally flat land presented few problems, though a low ridge was pierced by a shallow cutting and short tunnel at Curdworth. For boaters, this once represented a peaceful interlude after the hustle and bustle of Birmingham, but all that changed with the building of the M42. There is, however, one pleasing oddity near the end of the line. The canal was built close to Drayton Manor, home to Sir Robert Peel who, before he achieved fame as a politician, made a fortune in textiles and actually built a three-storey water-powered cotton mill beside the canal at Fazeley Junction. Today, however, the manor site is home to a park and zoo, but it does have its own, unique accommodation bridge. The wooden walkway is suspended between two crenellated towers, creating a very odd, imitation Gothic structure. The end of the line is overlooked by an elegant, double-fronted junction house.

*The Birmingham & Fazeley had to take over completion of the line of the Coventry Canal. Traffic on the two canals was overseen from the offices in Fazeley Junction House with its imposing two-storey bay front.*

*Canal engineers found ingenious solutions to everyday problems, in this case where to store the stop planks that fit into grooves on the bank to isolate a section of canal. An alcove in the bridge abutment at Curdworth provides the ideal, dry storage area.*

*The Cincinnati Works beside the Birmingham & Fazeley deserves a special word of praise as one of the first modern factories to open up to the canal and plant the bank with flowers and shrubs.*

*Fazeley became a centre of the cotton industry when Sir Robert Peel established mills here in the 1790s, making use of canal connections. This, however, is Tolson's Mill of 1883 used for weaving heavy-duty cloths.*

*More of a folly than a practical canal bridge, this extraordinary structure has rather more to do with pleasing the landowner of nearby Drayton Park Manor than it does with the canal.*

# 6. Across the Pennines

The most ambitious of all the canal schemes brought forward in the early years was undoubtedly that of the Leeds & Liverpool. As finally constructed, it was just over 127 miles long, was built with broad locks and in its cross-country course it had somehow to cope with the inconvenient fact that the Pennine hills sat right across a straight line drawn from Leeds to Liverpool. As if that were not enough, the project was promoted not by one unified committee but by two recruited at the two ends of the line: they were very far from agreement on anything at all. The first public meeting to discuss the plan was held in July 1766, but it was only after a great deal of bad-tempered wrangling that the Leeds committee reached agreement with their Liverpool counterpart, and a parliamentary act was obtained in 1770.

If they believed their troubles were then over, they were greatly mistaken. Original estimates suggested with dubious accuracy that the whole canal could be completed for a sum of £259,777 and that there would be no obstacles in the way of a swift and successful conclusion. Alas, the final bill came to about £1,200,000 and the grand opening, when a flotilla of boats left Leeds and made a through journey to Liverpool for the very first time, took place in October, 1816. Over that time, the plans for the line were to go through many changes, particularly at the Lancashire end where disagreements about the preferred route were the fiercest. In the circumstances, one can hardly look for complete uniformity, but even so it comes as something of a surprise to find that not even the locks are the same size throughout the canal. All are 14ft 3in wide and from Leeds to Wigan are 62ft long, but they gain an extra 10ft in length for the remainder of the line to Liverpool. It is necessary to look back at the origins of the canal to understand this strange anomaly.

The idea for the canal originated in Yorkshire, where the engineer John Longbotham surveyed a likely route at his own expense and then, with the financial backing of a Bradford wool merchant John Hustler, brought the scheme forward to the public. A Yorkshire committee was formed and only after that was established was the second committee recruited in Liverpool. Almost from the first there were disagreements. Longbotham's route started with a junction with the Aire & Calder Navigation in Leeds then followed the Aire valley to Gargrave. There it crossed the watershed heading for Colne. The Lancashire end of the route was devised with ease of engineering as the prime concern, swinging in a vast curve down the valleys of the Lancashire Calder and the Ribble before reaching the comfortably flat land for a direct route through Ormskirk to Liverpool. Simply viewed in engineering terms this course made sense, if the main object was to reduce extensive earthworks to a minimum in the Brindley manner. What it failed to do, however, was to meet the trading needs of the Lancashire interest, for it missed out important centres, such as the rapidly growing cotton towns of Blackburn and Burnley. The Yorkshire proposal, that this could be dealt with by building branches at some later date, was not met with any great enthusiasm. The Liverpool committee commissioned their own engineers to survey a different line through Lancashire, which met their special needs, but as it also attempted to avoid physical obstacles it would have added a further seventeen miles to an already long canal. Arbitration was called for and the parties consulted James Brindley, who sent his assistant Robert Whitworth to report on the matter. He got as far as Burnley, at which point he discovered that the Lancashire engineers were out in their levels by an astonishing thirty-five feet, and therefore proclaimed them guilty of gross incompetence and declared in favour of Longbotham.

It did not end there, for the Lancashire interest had their route surveyed all over again, but finally gave up the fight when the Yorkshire committee agreed to another of their demands that work should begin simultaneously at both ends, rather than simply heading west out of Leeds. It was not a happy compromise, and the Liverpool interest soon found ways of pressing their own concerns. Their most important objective was in gaining access to the coalfields around Wigan, and they had very little interest in anything to the east of there. They, therefore, wanted a canal that could accommodate Mersey barges, just as the Bridgewater had done, and built their locks accordingly. Over in Leeds, however, there was little interest in Mersey boats; they saw traffic in terms of the keels of the Aire & Calder, which were shorter. So they were quite happy to build shorter locks, and through traffic was to be handled by the company's own specially built short boats. This difference in planning reflects the clash of interests, but was not quite as bizarre as it now seems. At this stage no one was thinking of connecting to a national canal network, and the fact that the narrow boats of the Midlands would not be able to use the canal was not considered significant. There was one real curiosity in the original scheme, which called for an aqueduct across the       Navigation. When the plans were published, it was soon clear that it would be too low to allow masted vessels on the Douglas to pass underneath. The Leeds & Liverpool blithely proposed building a deep side cutting beside the existing line of the Douglas, with locks providing access at either end. Astonishingly, the Douglas were happy to agree to this absurd proposal. They did so because the plan also called for a branch from the new canal down to the Douglas, which would provide a link to the Ribble and on to Preston. In attempting to juggle so many different interests the Leeds & Liverpool risked pleasing none. As none of the backers felt that their particular needs were being completely answered, there was no rush to reinvest when financial difficulties arose.

As construction dawdled along over the years and engineers came and went, so there were to be numerous changes to the line. Longbotham was forced to resign in 1775 and was replaced by Richard Owen who lasted until 1782 when all work stopped due to lack of funds. A new act was passed in 1790 which not only authorized the raising of new capital, but brought the line back to what the

Liverpool men had always wanted in the first place. It was then no longer possible to think of the canal in isolation and connections were planned to join the Bridgewater extension at Leigh and to meet the newly promoted Lancaster Canal. In fact, in order to speed up the completion of a through line, it was proposed to use part of the southern end of the Lancaster. Work began again under Whitworth, and when he died in 1799 his place was taken by Samuel Fletcher.

The Leeds & Liverpool may have been an early canal, in that it was begun near the beginning of the canal age, but as so many were involved in its construction, over such a long period of time, it cannot be said to have a single, coherent identity in the way that say a Brindley canal has. However, in its overall planning one can still see that Longbotham's ideas lie at the heart of it. A direct route between the two termini would have been roughly sixty-five miles long. The line, as built, was almost twice that; Brindley himself could not have done better. The Pennines were not so much conquered as avoided. This might make one think that Longbotham was a somewhat timid engineer, but he was working within the context of the available technology of the time and he was confronted by extremely difficult terrain. He was building a broad canal, not a narrow one, so that even on level sections his work force were required to excavate twice as much material as Brindley's navvies working further south. He faced major difficulties right at the start, coping with the steep gradient of the Aire valley, and his solutions are still awe-inspiring. Therefore it is only fitting when looking at the canal to start at Leeds, where work began under Longbotham's direction.

*The small Leeds & Liverpool office in Leeds has been executed with care. The neatly carved arches round the window are carried down to floor level to give a sense of height to what could otherwise seem a rather squat building.*

As with other canals, the junction with a river navigation was a natural centre for development, doubly so in this case as the two met in the heart of an already thriving industrial and commercial town. Leeds continued to grow, developing from town to city, and it is inevitable that any such central area would change remarkably in the course of two centuries. The coming of the railways had a dramatic impact, with lines sweeping into City Station on high banks and viaducts, the station buildings themselves perched above the River Aire, which thunders underneath through gloomy arches. The navigable cut of the Aire & Calder meets the canal itself at a lock just above Leeds Bridge, a busy area of wharves and warehouses, where steam cranes could still be seen unloading coal as recently as the 1960s. Now the whole area has been redeveloped in the fashion of the 1980s and 1990s, with warehouses converted to offices and apartments, and new developments that borrow architectural ideas from the old squeezed in between. It has all been a great success in revitalizing what had become a very run down area, and it is now a part of Leeds where people congregate on a sunny day simply to enjoy the watery charms of river and canal. A charming little survivor is the Leeds company office to be found, appropriately, close to Office Lock. It could be thought rather pretentious to give such a modestly-sized building a grand classical style, but the anonymous architect had a good eye for proportions, and the masons have produced exemplary ashlar for the facade, well-carved mouldings and attractive lettering. It ends up looking quietly dignified. It is easy to miss among the more clamorous buildings that have appeared in the wharf area – the Royal Armouries Museum, which has little to do with the

*As in Birmingham, Leeds has rediscovered its canal and it now provides a focus for city centre development. In the background is the long viaduct carrying the railway into City Station.*

canal, and Tetley's Brewery Wharf, which at least acknowledges the importance of water transport in the development of the industry.

Newer developments are left behind as the canal begins its slow climb up through six locks, bunched quite close together with the Aire never very far away. The line of the canal has been largely dictated by the natural line of the river. Where the river flows straight, the canal follows suit; if it wanders off on a sweeping curve, the good neighbour keeps in step, meandering alongside. At first the overwhelming impression is of industry crowding in on the canal and it is tempting to see this as just another example of industrialists jostling for a place by an excellent new transport system. That is not, by any means, always the case. When the canal was built, mills and factories were water powered, and the main attraction in selecting a site was most likely to be the fast flowing waters of the Aire. The steep gradient that caused such headaches to Longbotham was just what the industrialists admired. The best known of the mills is at Armley which has its origins back in the sixteenth century when it was used both for fulling, part of the final processing of woollen cloth, and for grinding corn. It was rebuilt for the first time in 1788 when it was claimed to be the world's largest fulling mill and other processes were added, from the opposite end of the manufacturing process – scribbling and carding the raw wool. Development continued throughout the nineteenth century and today it houses a splendid industrial museum. Armley Mills made use of canal transport because it was available close at hand, but it was here long before the canal arrived.

There are other reminders along the way that Leeds was not an Industrial Revolution parvenu. The canal passes the ruins of the twelfth century Cistercian Abbey at Kirkstall, its stonework blackened by smoke, some of which came from the nearby forge, itself a successful enterprise of the seventeenth century. It all serves as a reminder that this is a canal that was built through a well-established industrial world; it was not going to be short of customers. Yet in spite of this, the canal itself provides a surprisingly green corridor out through the Leeds suburbs.

All the time, the canal is continuing its climb up the Aire valley – it has already reached lock number seven by Kirkstall. A defining feature of this canal is that it seldom moves very far from the millstone grit area, ensuring an abundance of good building stone. It is not a stone that takes readily to delicate embellishments, but it is quarried in large blocks which makes it very suitable for engineering works, such as lock chambers and bridges. It is equally suitable for buildings where durability is more important than ornamentation, as in warehouses and stable blocks. In smaller structures, such as lock cottages, it can give a rather dour, lumpish finish. Travelling the canal, one can see how the lock cottages share the same basic use of materials with the older farm buildings. The walls are of random rubble, that is, built of roughly cut stones of different sizes, laid in irregular courses. Dressed stones are used at quoins and lintels where strict verticals and horizontals are needed. Roofs were probably all originally stone slate, something of a misnomer, as these are flat plates of sandstone not slate, heavy but durable. This roofing material was available locally, and with transport costs high before the canal was completed, local materials were always preferred. Later on, however,

*Canalside housing at Rodley shows the characteristics of buildings constructed from local gritstone: large stone blocks for walls and roughly carved slabs for door and window surrounds. The same use of material can be seen along much of the canal.*

when replacements were called for, actual slates could be brought by boat at low cost. Although it is so readily available, building in stone is always expensive and the Leeds & Liverpool was never rich, and often all but bankrupt. So there was an incentive from the start to look for the cheapest option.

Bridges come in three main varieties along this section of the canal. Road bridges are solid, gritstone structures, again built of random rubble with dressed stone used for arches and parapets. Locks are often supplied with the simplest of foot bridges, consisting of single squared baulks of timber, with hand rails set out at an angle at the sides to fit the human figure – wider in the middle than at the feet. Elsewhere moveable bridges predominate. Being a wide canal, there was no possibility of building lift bridges as on the Oxford, the platform would have been too heavy to raise without a mechanical aid, so swing bridges were built instead. These, however, present their own problems; they have a tendency for the platform end to droop under its own weight so that it sits hard down on its stone recess instead of sliding smoothly across. This is compensated for by screw-threaded iron ties. If the bridge is to work well, these need to be checked regularly and adjusted, and the pivot kept well greased. Even then, they provide an unwelcome interruption to boat crews.

It is not just bridges that show interesting variations along the way. Locks were fitted with conventional gate and ground paddles, which are lifted and lowered by the usual rack and pinion gear, while others are worked directly through a vertical screw. Some

*A typical bridge across a lock, this example from Barrowford is simplicity itself – just a squared block of timber with handrails.*

*As all who travel the Leeds & Liverpool become aware, swing bridges are a common sight on the canal. At least this one near Kildwick gives boaters time to pause and admire the Pennine scenery.*

*Unusual features at some locks are the 'jack cloughs'. To move the ground paddles, the levers are lifted. More conventional paddle gear can be seen on the gates.*

ground paddles were also of the type known as 'jack cloughs', in which the paddle is swung across the face of the culvert by means of a lever worked from the top of the lock. Some gates also had radial cloughs, in which the paddle moves horizontally worked by rack and pinion on the top of the gate. There is probably no canal in the country with a greater variety of means for letting water into and out of a lock. Another curious feature is the lack of ladders in many lock chambers. Leeds & Liverpool boatmen climbed out via the lock gates, which had rungs fitted into the timber frame.

At the Forge locks to the west of Kirkstall, the pace of the climb begins to quicken. Altogether, the canal had to be lifted to a summit over 250ft above the river at Leeds. Longbotham decided, very sensibly, to make a series of leaps to reach a long pound, rather than to create a long stagger of single locks. So locks were grouped into double-risers, three-lock staircases and a five-lock staircase to complete the climb to a seventeen-mile pound. The first two sets of three-lock staircases come quite close together as the canal swings round the wooded hill, known as 'The Nosegay' This is quite unlike the contour cutting of the Brindley canals, where detours were made in order to preserve a level. Here, the canal climbs as it turns. The only alternative would have been a cutting through the hill, but the height would still have had to have been gained somewhere. This turns out to be the perfect compromise, for the extra length of canal that had to be cut in order to get round the hill was a far better option than taking on the expense and effort of building extensive earthworks. Having rounded the hill, Longbotham had the luxury of a long pound through the mill town of Shipley. There, what appears to be a short arm or basin turns away to the south in the shadow of a large warehouse complex. This is, in fact, all that remains of the Bradford Canal. It was promoted at the same time as the Leeds & Liverpool, with Longbotham again employed as Chief Engineer. Work began in 1771 and three years later the $3\frac{1}{2}$m long canal with its ten locks was open from there to Bradford. There was an extensive limestone traffic from Pennine quarries in the early years, but by the middle of the nineteenth century a severe water shortage forced a closure. The quarry owners were dismayed, protested loudly and the canal was reopened, sold to the Leeds & Liverpool in 1878 and prospered for a time. It did not last and in 1922 it was closed for good, filled in apart from this short arm. Only the nineteenth-century warehouses hint at more successful days.

One of Britain's best-known industrial towns stands beside the canal beyond Shipley. Sir Titus Salt built a vast mill complex for manufacturing mohair beside the Aire, hence the name, Saltaire. Although there is a considerable wharf area, the main attraction for Salt when he came here in the 1850s was the new railway that had opened in 1848. The mill itself sits conveniently between these two transport routes. The countryside of the Aire valley also had a part to play in the selection of the site, for Salt wanted to escape from the filth, grime and slums of Bradford. He built a model town for his workforce, and equipped it with every desirable amenity – hospital, library, church, park, almshouses and shops. One item he did not consider desirable, and which was never built, was a pub. Saltaire remains much as it was when built, and it is still possible to see how houses were graded – not just by size, but by details such as the style of window and the type of front door to proclaim the status of the occupants. Apart from being intrinsically interesting, it is worth pausing to look at the contrast between Saltaire's industrial buildings and houses and those of an earlier age. On the canal itself, warehouses, maintenance buildings and lock cottages use the local vernacular, employing local masons and builders who worked to old, familiar patterns. Saltaire shows the hand of the architect rather than the jobbing builder, consciously designed so that motifs are repeated to give a sense of unity. The selected style has nothing to do with Yorkshire and textile manufacture, but draws its inspiration from Italy – even the factory chimney is made to look like a campanile. It is all more sophisticated than the canal buildings, but not necessarily more satisfying to the eye; there is a great deal to say in favour of local styles and local materials as they harmonize with the landscape. The correlation between the rough stone used in building walls and bridges and the outcrops that form craggy edges to the surrounding hills is plain for all to see.

The canal then gathers itself for a climb up through the Dowley Gap, where the hills crowd together. The valley floor is narrow with no room for manoeuvre, and as the river turns away to the south, hugging the hillside, the canal is squeezed out and has to cross to the northern bank. Nothing fancy was required and nothing fancy provided, just a plain stone aqueduct carried on seven arches that strides across the valley floor. Once across the river, the towpath also changes sides and the giant steps appear; firstly, a two-lock riser lifts the canal by 18ft 2in, soon followed by a three-lock staircase adding a further 29ft 11ins and culminating in the famous Bingley Five Rise, raising the canal by a massive 60ft. No one needs to be a canal expert to be impressed

by this five-lock staircase, but the details are also interesting. The first thing to note is the quality of the stone work. The massive blocks that line the wharf at the foot of the staircase are carried on up as coping for the wing wall of the bottom lock. All the work around the locks shows the same skilled masons' work, with well-squared blocks, firmly bonded to withstand the considerable pressures exerted by such a large head of water. The same careful work can be seen in the steps at the lock-side and in the cobbled culverts of the overspill weirs. The bottom gates of each lock are crossed by the usual timber-baulk bridge. The control of water through this system was all-important – improper use could lead to a massive haemorrhage from the long pound above the locks. So there is both a substantial lock cottage at the top and a smaller lobby at the bottom. The cottage itself is a late arrival, constructed out of recycled stone from a warehouse demolition at the Liverpool end.

Above Bingley almost everything changes. The canal no longer mimics every twist and turn of the wayward Aire, but keeps to a level by hugging the hillside to the north of the river, looking out over the broad valley floor of Airedale. This whole section is a great tribute to Longbotham's surveying skills. The gradient of the Aire has eased and the river flows more placidly. By leaping to a point on the hillside well above the Aire, he was able to stay on the same contour for seventeen miles, as canal level and river level slowly converged. It would provide a long, interrupted stretch were it not for the ubiquitous swing bridges. The course still runs up Airedale and there are still constant reminders of the woollen industry and the use it made of the canal. Silsden, confusingly, has two Canal Mills, each with its own wharf. There are also reminders of the pre-factory age in villages such as Kildwick with its venerable bridge over the river, and overlooked by stately Kildwick Hall which, like so many buildings using the local gritstone, presents a rather dour face to the world.

Longbotham had brought the canal as far as Skipton by April 1773, and shortly after that he resigned, apparently under pressure from the Canal Committee who felt he was devoting insufficient time to their project. Considering the progress that was made under his direction and the great works already completed, they may well have come to regret their impatience. Work on the canal would never proceed at such a pace again. Skipton was one of the key locations along the canal. The town stands at a geological boundary, where the gritstone meets the limestone that dominates so much of the Yorkshire Dales. Limestone had many uses: it could be burned in kilns to produce lime, which was used as a fertiliser. It was particularly useful in the millstone grit country where the soil is poor, and the stone was sent to canalside limekilns, many of which can still be seen along the way, though the most impressive set of all, built beside the Bradford Canal, have long since been demolished. The stone was also used as a flux in the blast furnaces of the iron industry.

There were, and are, extensive quarries at Haw Bank, near Embsay to the east of Skipton, on land owned by Lord Thanet. In 1772, a separate act was passed for a short branch canal that would pass, moat-like, under the walls of Skipton Castle to connect with a waggon road from the quarries. It was later extended, an incredibly difficult job which involved hacking a way through the solid rock on which the castle was built to create what is now known as the Springs Branch. It ended in hundred foot high staithes, and one can still see the chutes down which the limestone was tipped from trucks on the quarry tramway down to the waiting boats.

For a short canal, just half a mile long, it is full of interest, not least because a walk down its towpath shows how man has played with the natural forces of water for his own advantage. There are three quite separate levels here: the Haw Beck has been dammed in its upper reaches to supply a leat running to the High Corn Mill; below that is the stream itself and the canal.

Skipton grew up as a market town sheltering under the protection of the castle walls – a place where the broad market square was surrounded by little alleys and approached by packhorse routes from the surrounding districts. The arrival of the canal changed its character, or rather grafted a new, vigorous shoot onto the old stock. The canal not only took limestone out, it brought coal in, and development soon followed. The new enterprises looked both east and west, to Yorkshire and to Lancashire, building steam powered mills, dyehouses and warehouses, dealing at first in wool, but later converting to cotton. Canalside Belle Vue Mills showed a typical pattern of development. Built in 1828 for worsted spinning and weaving, it was soon converted for cotton spinning, weaving and dyeing. The weaving sheds and spinning blocks of the old mills line the canal and all around them is the new Skipton. Gone is the higgledy-piggledy random pattern of alleys and lanes that seemed to have grown organically through the centuries, and in their place came the planned terraces of uniform housing laid out on a neat grid. This was the Skipton that developed when the Industrial Revolution floated into town, courtesy of the Leeds & Liverpool Canal. This is a more lasting legacy than the old town wharf, with its warehouse now converted into a shop, and its hand cranes preserved as decorative items, not intended for use.

Leaving Skipton, the canal begins its journey through the hilly countryside, where farm pasture is divided up by drystone walls, which straggle on up above the valley fields to the rough moorland and then disappear over the skyline. This is beautiful country, with the canal skirting the edge of the Yorkshire Dales National Park. But the scenery that delights holiday makers – including holiday boaters – must have been a nightmare for surveyors. Today we have the benefit of detailed Ordnance Survey maps, with contour lines drawn in to give an accurate picture of the terrain. They enjoyed no such luxury. What we can see by looking at the modern map is a seemingly hopeless muddle of hillocks and hollows through which, somehow, the canal had to find its way. At first the route was quite easy, still staying with the Aire valley.

*The Springs branch now seems a romantic backwater running between Skipton church and the former Leatt corn mill. It was once a thriving waterway, however, carrying boats loaded with limestone from quarries in the hills.*

But the river has its origins in the hills to the north, while the canal has to head south west towards Liverpool. The steady climb continues, out past Gargrave and then the canal turns at last, crossing the Aire on a three-arched aqueduct. Once across the river, the towpath changes sides, and the turnover bridge builders were profligate with their materials, providing two very long approach ramps for the horses. Up ahead, the hills seem ever more daunting and there is a climb of fifty-six feet through the six Bank Newton locks before the canal goes into convulsions, winding in extravagant loops through the knobbly landscape. So severe are the bends that the Company had to install rollers set on high, stout wooden posts to guide the tow rope, otherwise the line would cut across the curve, dragging the boat into the bank. It perhaps gives some idea of what this countryside is like to know that the towpath also forms part of the Pennine Way long-distance footpath.

The wriggling comes to an end near East Marton, where road improvements resulted in a higher level route through the village. Instead of building an entirely new bridge, the existing bridge was heightened by building a second arch above the first. One can still see how the stonework of the two bridges has been keyed in. The canal passes through some of the most open countryside of its route until it reaches the three Greenberfield locks that lift it up to a summit, about forty-one miles from the start at Leeds. There are few, if any, more delightful lock flights than this. The scenery is inspiring, the views across the hills magnificent and the immediate surroundings of the canal fit perfectly into the wider picture. The

*The canal crosses the Aire near Gargrave on a plain but neat aqueduct, carried on three elliptical arches. There is just a hint of decoration in the pillars and well-defined string-course.*

*The Pennine Way makes use of the towpath of the canal for a short distance near Barnoldswick. The building behind the wall has sandstone 'slates' on the roof.*

towpath is bordered by a drystone wall, and the locks climb round the smooth, grassy shoulder of a hill. At the top is the neat, stone lock cottage, its only ornament a little sundial, dated 1824. We are not in fact seeing the Greenberfield locks as they were built at all. Originally there was a three-lock staircase here, but it was thought to be wasting water, so the present locks were built in 1820. It helped in conserving water, but was not enough. Water supply to the short summit was a perennial problem, which had still not been fully resolved even by the end of the nineteenth century. Drastic measures were needed so a new reservoir was constructed at Winterburn, north of Gargrave, with water carried by pipeline for $8\frac{1}{2}$ miles to the Winterburn Discharge control building at the locks, which still carries the date when the work was completed, 1893.

The canal now crosses from Yorkshire into Lancashire and begins to enter the cotton kingdom. Before reaching it, however, the engineers had to tackle a ridge that lay across the line, on top of which perched the village of Foulridge. They must have thought it aptly named, for no part of the canal was to cause more trouble. Longbotham had planned to go round the ridge, but when Whitworth took over as work restarted in 1789 after a seven-year stoppage when the money ran out, he recommended going straight ahead through a 1,640-yard tunnel. It was to be quite shallow, and Whitworth declared that 'it would be a small affair' and 'easier to make than most'. The method to be used was partly 'cut and cover', in which the ground was excavated down from the surface and then closed over to prevent the slippage that so often plagued deep cuttings. The central section was excavated in the conventional way. It was all to prove far more difficult than expected. The rock was rotten and crumbling, and it seemed that as soon as an area was dug, the sides would collapse in again. In the event it was not ready until 1796. However, that was not to be the end of the story; it collapsed in 1824, again in 1843 and yet again in 1902, each time being rebuilt. This whole Foulridge area was a bustle of activity for many years, with a succession of reservoirs being constructed to supply the ever-thirsty summit, beginning in 1788 with the Lower Foulridge reservoir. In this area one does not see the canal as originally planned, but rather a canal that was forced to develop and evolve over the years to answer the specific problems created by having a short summit through difficult ground.

*The wharf at Foulridge, by the tunnel entrance. It shows clearly how the same styles and materials were used in the canal buildings as in the pub and houses.*

The summit ends at Barrowford, where seven locks drop the canal down by nearly 70ft. If it seems that locks, lock cottage and warehouse all belong in this setting, then it may be due in part to the fact that the building stone came from a quarry less than a mile from the canal. The route then heads out through the tightly packed towns and villages that developed with the growth of the cotton industry. The first of these, Nelson, was originally called Marsden and, like the Yorkshire Marsden, began life as a woollen town, only turning to cotton in the 1850s. But it was as a cotton town that Nelson thrived, with heavy development along the canal. By now the idea of the canal as an axis for development had been well established. Many of these mills were built on spec as 'room and power' mills, where the owners leased out the space, steam engine and line shafting to manufacturers, confident that there would be no shortage of takers on such a site.

The next section of the route is particularly interesting, for it shows how much has changed in the years since the canal had first been planned. The original route had headed north for an easy line along the Ribble valley. Whitworth proposed heading for Burnley, tackling the main obstacles head on. A rather wandering line brought the canal to the edge of the Calder valley from whence it strode ahead on a massive embankment, 46ft high and $\frac{3}{4}$ mile long and crossing the river on an aqueduct that is, in effect, an arch piercing the high bank. Much of the material that was used in building up the bank came from excavations to the south west, where the high ground was pierced by deep cuttings and a 559 yard long tunnel. More recently, the route through the tunnel was joined by the railway, using bank and viaduct and the M65, which now dominates the area. The canal embankment is a dramatic feature overlooking the town and once offering what L.T.C. Rolt described as the finest industrial view in the country – not any more. Burnley has removed most of the reminders of its industrial past from the town centre, so that today the bank, known exaggeratedly as The Burnley Mile, soars over shopping precincts and road junctions. At the southern end, however, the canal swings round past the maintenance yard to enter an area of intensive development, with both mills and houses for the textile workers crowding in on the waterway. It is not difficult to guess the age of some of the mills – the name 'Trafalgar Mill' for example, gives more than a hint of just when it was built. Many are early nineteenth century, and all are post-canal. On the towpath side, there are wharf areas, some of them canopied to provide cover, while on the opposite side, where the water laps at the factory walls, one can still see the massive iron mooring rings below the hoist covers. Everything points to the fact that this was a vital part of the industrial development of Lancashire.

The route winds its way through cotton towns and cotton villages. By taking the high level route through Burnley, the canal is able to maintain a level for thirteen miles from Barrowford to the next flight of six locks at Blackburn. One soon begins to notice real changes of character as the millstone grit, which has been such a constant companion, gives way to a softer sandstone. As a result, brick begins to vie with stone as the preferred building material. There are still reminders of former glories in the Eanam canal wharf and basin in Blackburn, where coal was unloaded for the mills. Here old warehouses still stand, together with stables and wharf manager's house, but

*Gritstone and sandstone are abundantly available, but they are not hard-wearing. Tow ropes have cut deep grooves into the abutments of this bridge near Burnley.*

Blackburn turned away from the canal, and many of the old buildings along the route have been demolished. There has been a change of heart recently, but there are few traces on the ground to show what effect the coming of the canal had on the town but, as in Birmingham, old maps have a clearer message. Old Blackburn was based on the river Darwen, which supplied power for the early mills. The canal ignored all this, passing high over the river on a single-arched aqueduct and passing well to the south of the original town. A map of 1824 shows what was, in effect, a separate village growing up along the canal and separated from old Blackburn by open country. It was not until well into the nineteenth century that the two settlements expanded and joined to form the one town we see today. The names tell their own story on the map – Navigation Mill, Canal Mill, Canal Foundry and more.

The locks at Johnson's Hillock are a serious rival to Greenberfield for the 'most attractive' award. The hillock is there, with a crown of trees, and round it the canal sways, falling through seven locks. This is also an important point in the complex history of the Leeds & Liverpool. When work was begun, the line was laid down with little thought either for rivals or for possible later connections, but thanks to the long delays, by the time work was restarted the canal map was beginning to fill up. The original plan had called for connections with the Douglas Navigation, which would give access to Preston. Then, in 1792, the newly formed Lancaster Canal Co. set out their line, which would actually cross the Ribble to the west of Preston to meet the Leeds & Liverpool near Eccleston. This would have involved the construction of an immense, and immensely expensive, aqueduct. As with so many canal companies, relations began in mutual suspicion, and it took some time to recognize that cooperation would be to their mutual advantage. It was decided to bring the Lancaster to a temporary halt at Preston, and the route south would be continued via a tramway to Walton Summit, where the Lancaster would renew canal construction and take their line all the way to Wigan. The Leeds & Liverpool agreed to bring their line to Johnson's Hillock, and then to pay the Lancaster for the right to use their new route down to Wigan. The disused branch at the foot of the locks is all that remains of the

*Eanam wharf, Blackburn. The elements that make the warehouse buildings visually appealing all derive from practical functions: the rhythm of the façade with wide loading bays alternating with narrow windows, the canopy on iron supports, the covered hoists.*

Lancaster's route to Walton Summit. The arrangement lasted until the 1830s when the Lancaster abandoned its line south of Preston and sold the joint section to Wigan to the Leeds & Liverpool. It was only then that the latter could actually claim to own a canal that ran all the way from the Aire to the Mersey.

The canal, once it has escaped from the overwhelming presence of the M61, passes through an uncompromising landscape where robust mills and isolated farms nestle down against the wind in comfortable hollows, while the canal hugs the valley edge on its way to Wigan. This is the other former junction with the Lancaster, which was originally supposed to end further east at Westhoughton. There is a sharp bend down to the Wigan locks, and only a short stump remains of the earlier route. This is by far the most heavily locked section of the canal with twenty-one broad locks in a continuous flight which, with two more isolated locks, give a total fall of almost 215ft. At the foot of the main flight is the Leigh Branch, opened in 1820 to connect directly at Leigh with a branch of the Bridgewater Canal, arriving from Worsley in the south. Now the Leeds & Liverpool was connected to the great Midlands network. The Leigh branch had been built with short locks, but requests from narrow boat users, notably Pickford's, resulted in them being extended, together with the two bottom Wigan locks to provide a route to Liverpool.

Wigan itself acquired even greater importance than it had as the Leeds & Liverpool-Lancaster junction, it was also the trans-shipment point between the seventy-foot narrow boats and the short boats from the east. This was to develop into one of the busiest sections on the whole canal, for it was also the hub from

*A flight of twenty-one broad locks drops the canal down to Wigan, a town which with its industries and coalfield held the key to development of the canal at the Lancashire end.*

which tramways radiated out to the surrounding collieries. Many of these were later taken over and adapted as steam railways and something of the extent of the system can be gauged from modern maps which show the large numbers of working and disused lines centred on Wigan. It is no surprise to find both a maintenance yard and a substantial canal basin at the foot of the locks, at the area now known as Wigan Pier. There is some doubt about the nature of the pier itself. There are those who claim it was no more than an Orwellian joke and others who claim that it applied to the hump on the wharf – all that remains of old coal staithes. But from September 1808, the canal company began running a daily packet boat that plied between here and Liverpool, and passengers boarded at the pier. The present Wigan Pier museum complex is based on the basin. The oldest buildings are of stone, and include a warehouse with double-pitched roof and two shipping holes, so that boats could slide through the arches to be loaded through trapdoors. More stone buildings line the wharf, the most imposing having prominent keystones over loading bays and arches and weather-boarded hoist covers, cantilevered out over the canal. Further to the west, the next range of warehouses is of later date, built in brick, with round-headed windows, providing the extra strength that the old builders could obtain by using massive stone lintels. Now the hoist covers rise above the wharf, rather than over the water.

The canal heads west along the Douglas valley, on what was once known as the Upper Douglas Navigation, for we are now back with the early construction at the Liverpool end. In 1777, the whole route had been opened from Liverpool to Wigan, but the journey from Gathurst to Wigan was along the river, not by canal. River and canal were linked by a lock at the present Dean Locks, which were built three years

*This scene on the Leigh Arm looks more like the Fens than industrial Lancashire, but these are mining flashes created by subsidence not natural lakes.*

*A short branch at Wigan Pier leads to a typical nineteenth-century cotton mill. Power for Trencherfield Mill came from an immense four-cylinder steam engine introduced in 1907, with a great appetite for coal carried by canal.*

later, when the present line was open, bypassing the river altogether. This whole area around Wigan shows the canal company constantly changing its mind over which way to go, partly as a response to difficulties encountered in the landscape, but more often because the arrival of new canal proposals caused old plans to be rethought. In the end it was all very different from what Longbotham had envisaged. He was going to miss Wigan altogether and take a roundabout route that would pass through Walton Summit to join the Ribble valley. A start to the Longbotham line was made at Parbold but rapidly abandoned, and all that remains is a stumpy little arm.

Even with the arrival of the Lancaster on the scene, the Douglas was still thought of as providing an important link through to the Ribble. The Leeds & Liverpool set about improvements by what was, quite correctly, known as the Lower Douglas Navigation. There was a wholly canalized section, running from Burscough for seven miles to Tarleton Lock which gave access to the tidal river. The canal section is now known as the Rufford Branch. The junction bridge is very handsome and dated 1816,

*At Burscough Junction the Rufford branch leaves the main line of the Leeds & Liverpool for a connection with the River Douglas. The bridge carrying the towpath over the branch has unusually long approach ramps even for a junction bridge.*

but the branch itself was actually opened by 1781. There is a quick scuttle downhill through four locks, then just three more locks before the river lock is reached.

From this point, the canal begins its final swing south towards Liverpool, across a largely flat landscape that presented few problems for the engineers and builders. For once, it was actually constructed along the line set out in the original act. Instead of the tight turns of the hilly eastern end, the canal here takes great, sweeping curves to keep a level and find the easiest route. One of the more extravagant bends can be found at Aintree, a spot well known to race-goers, for the famous Grand National course doubles back here at Canal Turn.

The final run towards Liverpool has been greatly altered over the years. The last section has been truncated, and the Pall Mall Wharves, which formed the original terminus, have gone. The change can be traced back to Liverpool dock improvements in the nineteenth century. Trafalgar Dock was built in 1836, to be followed by Salisbury Dock, built upstream of that in 1848. This new dock

*Burscough developed into an attractive canal settlement with interesting features including the rounded 'waggon corner' on the building on the right.*

opened out inland into first Collingwood Dock, then, furthest from the river, Stanley Dock. The latter was specifically designed to meet the needs of the canal company for it was equipped with the latest technology, for 'raising coal boxes out of barges and delivering them to ships'. This used hydraulic power, worked by pumping water up to the top of a tower known as an accumulator. The height of water created a considerable pressure, which could be applied through piping to move a ram in a cylinder, which could be used to work cranes and other machines. A new branch of the Leeds & Liverpool had to be built which dropped through four locks, and Stanley Dock became the new terminus. So, almost a century after it was first planned, the Leeds & Liverpool Canal was still involved in applying the latest technology to the work of moving cargo by water.

*The structures on the Rufford branch have the same characteristics as those of the main line. The curve of this flight of stone steps adds to the appeal of the lock scene.*

*The Leeds & Liverpool ends its long journey with a short arm dropping down through four locks to Stanley Dock. The railway viaduct represents competition, carrying the line from Liverpool to Wigan.*

# 7. Loose Ends

Throughout the early years of canal building, promoters put forward plans for waterways to serve special areas and their particular needs. In general these were built to connect towns or industrial concerns to navigable rivers, though in some cases they would be extended by other new canals. The Erewash was brought further inland by means of the Cromford Canal; the Stroudwater was joined by the Thames & Severn to complete a route through the heart of the Cotswolds to unite those two important rivers. Some, such as the Chester Canal and Sir John Ramsden's Huddersfield Broad Canal, had to wait for decades before they were connected to new parts of the system. One canal, however, was built to serve just one town and a single trade, to carry salt from the area round Droitwich to the River Severn, and it was only forced to expand its links when faced by railway competition. The Droitwich Junction Canal was built in 1853, almost a century after work began on the original waterway.

Droitwich had been at the heart of a thriving salt trade since Roman times, when the town was known was known as Salinae. By the time that Domesday Book was compiled in the eleventh century, the town had ten brine pits and over two hundred evaporation pans for crystallizing out the salt. The biggest change came in the early eighteenth century when new deep borings brought a huge increase in production. Water transport seems to have had a role to play for many centuries and the River Salwarpe was certainly navigable in the medieval period. There are records of numerous attempts to improve navigation in the seventeenth and early eighteenth centuries, first by building flash locks and then pound locks. Looking at the convoluted course of the river it is difficult to imagine such efforts could ever have been very successful and whatever work was completed, there are no visible remains.

A much more enterprising idea was put forward in 1708 to create a pipeline of hollowed-out elm trunks to carry the brine to a new salt works to be established by the Severn at Hawford. Nothing came of it, and it was only with the advent of the canal age that real progress was made, with the passing of an Act in 1769, for a barge canal from the town, down the Salwarpe valley to the Severn.

Inevitably, it was James Brindley who was called in as Chief Engineer, and Joseph Priestley in his 1834 account of Britain's canals and river navigations described the Droitwich as his *chef-d'oeuvre* for 'the excellency of the works'. Excellent the works may have been, but it was a short canal that offered no serious difficulties. The route was obvious, closely following the line of the errant Salwarpe, while smoothing out the wrinkles, and as the canal remains to the south of the river, there was no need for aqueducts. The eight locks were built to take river craft, 64ft by 14ft 6ins and as the entire route was just under six miles, it was assumed that towing would be by man power, as it was on the Severn, and not horse power, and only the narrowest of towpaths was supplied.

It is now impossible to identify much in the way of original structures. The canal began at Chapel Bridge, which did actually have a chapel on top, but that was demolished just before work on the canal was begun. It was only the first of many changes. All salt extraction areas suffer from subsidence, and the canal was affected as much as anywhere else, resulting in a good deal of rebuilding. The greatest change, however, came with the arrival of the Junction Canal to the north, connecting the barge canal to the Worcester & Birmingham and the Midland canal system. This involved the construction of a large barge lock joining the two Droitwich canals, and the rebuilding of all the lower locks, extending their length to seventy-two feet for use by narrow boats. The towpath was widened for horse towing. So all that really remains of Brindley's canal is its typical wavering line and the positioning of the locks. The changes were not enough to keep the railways at bay. Traffic ended in 1918, the canal was officially abandoned in 1939 and it was left to fall derelict. The old barge canal, however, remained in water, which encouraged volunteers to consider restoration. Work began in 1970. Much has been done and most of the canal is again navigable, but modern road developments have chopped off the last section that would complete the link to the river.

*The little hire boat at Ladywood Lock shows that restorers have brought most of the Droitwich Canal back to life. The lock cottage, in spite of its traditional appearance, is a modern replacement.*

The most interesting features are the locks, but even here nothing is quite as it seems. Ladywood Lock, the first to be reached at the end of the long pound from Droitwich is extremely attractive. The lock cottage is a neat little building with dormer windows but is a mere twenty years old, replacing the original cottage, which was found to be unsafe. Similarly the traditional brick bridge over the tail of the lock proved inadequate for modern traffic and had to be replaced. This created a problem for restorers, who found there was not enough space for a conventional balance beam to swing, so new ones had to be supplied with a right-angled bend in the middle. The canal was, like the Staffs & Worcester, supplied with circular bye weirs, and there is a fine restored example by Lock Three in the flight. The Droitwich is still very attractive, but has had more face lifts than an ageing film star.

The final connection made to the Severn in the early period has a similar history in some ways in that it is still going through the same cycle of construction, success, dereliction and restoration. It differs from the Droitwich, however, in that it was extended very early on to create a through route from the west coast to the east. The Cotswolds seems an unlikely area for canal building, for today we think of the region as home to picturesque villages, specially designed with tourism in mind. However, a visitor to Stroud in the eighteenth century would have found a town sat at the meeting point of five valleys, and all down those valleys were woollen mills powered by rivers and streams, more than a hundred of them in all. This was the heartland of the thriving, prosperous West of England woollen industry and Stroud even gave a noun 'stroud' to the language, which can still be found in older dictionaries, defined as 'a blanket manufactured for barter or trade with the North American Indians', with the date of first appearance given as 1759.

This was not just a bustling industry, but one that already had a thriving export trade. It is no wonder that merchants and manufacturers dreamed of a direct water communication to the Severn and ultimately with what was then Britain's second largest port, Bristol. All kinds of schemes were proposed and an act was passed in 1730 for making the River Stroudwater, now known as the Frome, navigable. The idea was revived in 1759, but it was always doomed. The river supported too many mills, whose owners were determined to protect their water supplies. They were not about to share the precious commodity with anyone, no matter what the advantages. The third act of 1776 still speaks of 'making navigable the River Stroudwater' but makes clear that what the proprietors were empowered to do was to build a wholly artificial canal.

The canal was comparatively straightforward, built to accommodate the Severn trows, the sailing barges of the river, with locks allowing vessels up to 70ft long and 15ft 6in beam to use the waterway. Originally, there were thirteen locks, including the Framilode lock, which connected the canal to the river, but much of the canal is now derelict, having been closed in 1933. Over the years, developments and road improvements have swallowed up some of the features, but enough remains to give a good idea of how it was, and restoration work is already well under way. Because of the disappearance of some parts of the canal, for example under the M5, anyone wishing to see the remaining sections has to be selective. One of the more interesting areas can be reached by a walk along the towpath from Nutshell Bridge towards Stroud. This is a typically wide, high arched bridge, with a level parapet. At one end is a substantial house, keyed into the abutments, which suggests it had a canal connection, but it is clearly too grand for a lengthman's cottage and has no obvious commercial significance. It has been suggested that it was the gatehouse for the local cloth mill, from where traffic on both road and canal could be controlled. From here, one can see two railway bridges crossing the canal. That to the west carries the still active GWR line from Bristol to Gloucester, and the walk down the towpath brings one under the simple iron-girder bridge, built in the 1860s for the Stonehouse and Nailsworth Railway Co. With two railway companies competing with each other and with the canal, it is not too surprising that something had to give. The Stonehouse & Nailsworth faltered first, was taken over by the Midland and finally succumbed in 1947. It now carries a footpath and cycle track. It is ironic that the railway will probably never see locomotives again, while boats are returning to the canal it helped to kill. Continuing under Ryeford bridge, one is immediately aware of the River Frome, separated from the canal by no more than the width of the towpath. Indeed, the canal actually cut off a mill on the river, which still retains its water wheel, from the mill house and the two are now linked by a swing bridge. Further along, one reaches the biggest rise on the canal, the Ryeford double lock, with its two cavernous interconnected chambers. It was completed in 1779, although the adjoining lock cottage carries the date 1784. It is a plain, double-fronted house, with a single storey extension, which originally had a separate entrance, now blocked in. The façade is symmetrical, with two windows on the ground floor, three on the first, each topped with a segmented arch. It is just the sort of building that was being constructed at that time by the wealthier farmers for their workers or multiplied several times over in the new industrial villages and towns. The canal temporarily vanishes at Ebley Mill, a magnificent stone woollen mill of the early nineteenth century, built in a style reminiscent of a French chateau and now housing the local council offices. As on the Leeds & Liverpool, Ebley Mill made use of the canal, importing coal from the Forest of Dean, but there had been mills on the riverside site long before the appearance of the canal.

The Stroudwater ended at a large basin at Wallbridge on the edge of Stroud, but it was infilled in the 1950s, though the old company offices have survived. The headquarters building shows a suitably respectable face to the world at large, while the canal that paid for the grandeur has to make do with a ragged back end. The ashlar facade is unmistakeably Georgian with a regular array of tall sash windows, a pediment with an oval bull's eye window and the whole is topped by a cornice. Behind the symmetrical facade is a far less regular array, with walls of random rubble and a single storey extension to the main office building, tucked away out of sight. Scarcely had the Stroudwater been opened than plans were being laid to extend it eastward to the Thames. It was not, as one might think, the Stroudwater proprietors themselves who were the prime movers, but the Staffs & Worcester, eager to find a new market for Staffordshire coal. A route was surveyed in 1781

*The Thames & Severn at Bowbridge. The towpath provides a pleasant footpath up the Golden Valley, but the canal itself still awaits restoration.*

with the intention of creating a line to Cricklade. The surveyors, however, wisely decided that the upper Thames was an unreliable navigation, and preferred to make their connection further downstream at Lechlade. The line was originally surveyed by Robert Whitworth, after which he seems to have had little or nothing to do with the work, which became the responsibility of the Resident Engineer, Josiah Clowes. The first part of the route simply continues following the line of the Frome, but at some point it had to cross the watershed to the Thames. The climb up the valley steadily steepens, calling for twenty-eight locks in the first seven miles, twelve more in the next mile and a half and another seven packed into the last half mile. After that the engineers had had enough, having struggled to fit in all the locks needed to lift the canal 241ft from the start in Stroud, they still needed to climb another 250ft in less than half a mile if they were to clamber over the summit. It was clearly impossible, and the only practical solution was a tunnel, the longest yet attempted, 3,817 yards long, compared with 2,880 yards at Harecastle, and this was to be a broad tunnel, capable of passing Thames barges. From here things got easier, with a summit pound stretching $9\frac{1}{2}$ miles to Cirencester, though the last mile was in effect a branch to the town. The main line now began the descent to the Thames, a gentle fall with fifteen locks in $13\frac{1}{2}$ miles.

The decisions taken during the survey were to have long term effects for the canal's future. Little thought had been given to the problems of water supply. With locks to the west of the tunnel crowded so closely together, there was scarcely enough surplus in the intervening pounds to fill the next lock down the line, and there was a constant drain of water down from the summit. The problems were exacerbated by the geological nature of the region, where water seeps away through cracks in the underlying limestone. A quite different problem was that of traffic. There was no shortage of customers in the west, where mills lined the Golden Valley, a name that it may have won for its natural beauty but which could equally well reflect the considerable wealth generated by industry. On the Thames side of the canal, water shortages were less of a problem, but there were virtually no customers for the canal, merely a scatter of isolated farms and hamlets. The only trade consisted of through traffic to and from the Thames. Perhaps none of this seemed important when set against the huge difficulties faced in building the great Sapperton tunnel. In the end, it was water shortages and lack of cargoes that were to prove fatal.

Had the Thames & Severn been planned together with the Stroudwater from the first, then no doubt locks would have been uniform throughout its length. But the earlier canal had been designed specifically to take Severn trows. The new looked to Thames barges, and those trading up to Lechlade were roughly 88ft by 12ft, so locks on the new canal were longer and narrower, roughly 90ft by 13ft, than those on the old. Somewhere there had to be an interchange point, and an inland port was created at Brimscombe, $2\frac{1}{2}$ miles from the Wallbridge junction at Stroud. The eastern end was always the poor relation, and even though attempts were made to improve connections, with the completion of the North Wiltshire Canal down to Swindon, where it connected with the Wilts & Berks for a new Thames junction at Abingdon, trade declined. When E. Temple Thurston wrote his famous account of a canal journey aboard the *Flower of Gloster*, he met an old lengthman clearing the hedges to keep the towpath clear for horses that never came. The boatman explained to the author, 'He goes on working here day after day all year round, and every night he goes home he expects to find a letter from the Canal Company telling him he ain't wanted no longer. Don't tell him we haven't seen no barges, sur.' In fact, there was to be no more traffic over the summit after that year. The eastern end began its slow slide into dereliction and, by 1927, everything east of Chalford was officially closed. The line to the mills remained open a little longer, but by 1933 that too was gone, leaving only the Stroudwater to struggle on. It remained open until 1954. Now the slow work of restoration is under way, but not surprisingly most of the surviving features are to be found in the west, though even here much has been lost.

From the start at Stroud, the valley route is still lined with mills, though few now have any connection with textiles. Among the surviving features is a circular bye weir at Bowbridge: the design may be the work of Whitworth, who was taught by Brindley, and he may well have taken the idea from his old master. Sadly, the once important basin at Brimscombe has now been filled in, though there is one interesting feature nearby. The next lock up was built especially large, 90ft by 16ft, to enable the vessels from both the Thames and Severn to reach the company repair and boat building yard at Bourn. Perhaps the best spot to get the real flavour of the canal is at the old Chalford wharf. There has been a mill here since at least the sixteenth century, originally owned by Corpus Christi College, Oxford. The mill developed over the centuries, used at various times as wool mill, grist mill and silk mill. The present building has a main three-storey range striding across the millstream, and looks out over an extensive millpond. Next to it is the sixteenth-century clothier's house, at one time converted to an inn. Other mills of varying dates are all on view from the towpath of the canal, as is a curious circular stone building with a conical roof. This is the first of five round houses, once workmen's or lengthmen's cottages. Not all the company cottages are built in this way, so why was this odd shape chosen? It is true that it literally gives all round visibility, but it was neither very easy to construct nor easy to live in. One possible answer can be found in the local industry. Structures looking very much like this were built as wool stoves, for drying wool. One survivor can be seen a few miles away, close to the main road at South Woodchester. Its working days are over and it has been converted into a cottage, and now has a quite startling similarity to the Chalford round house. Was it a conscious effort to imitate a familiar structure, a task made easier by the fact that local masons were familiar with the construction methods? The records give no clue. Just past the cottage, the waterway enters what was known as 'the black gutter', an area of springs that could be tapped to feed the canal. There would be no water shortages downstream, no matter what happened further up the valley.

Beyond Chalford, the canal enters increasingly remote country in the deepening valley. It is still possible to follow the towpath through this beautiful countryside but, at the time of writing, lock chambers are empty and crumbling. This was the area that gave most problems to engineers. In the 1840s an attempt

*No-one seems quite certain why the Thames & Severn Company chose to build round houses such as this at Chalford, but, with its Gothic windows and conical roof, it is undeniably attractive.*

at water conservation was made by shortening the final seven locks to 70ft, and not all of these have survived. Emerging from the woodland, the canal passes under a road bridge and vanishes in front of the Daneway Inn. Looking more closely, part of a filled-in lock can be seen, the rest lost under the pub car park. There was originally a basin immediately below the lock, with warehouse and coal yard, and the winding road that climbs the hill to Sapperton village was built by the canal company for coal wagons. The Daneway itself was also a company building, which for a time housed some of the workers employed in excavating Sapperton tunnel. It was sold in 1807 and became The Bricklayers' Arms, a welcome sight to boatmen who had just legged a heavy barge for over two miles through the tunnel.

Sapperton tunnel is not merely the most impressive engineering feature on the canal, it is arguably the most impressive canal tunnel in Britain. In length it is surpassed by just one, Standedge on the Huddersfield Canal, but that is a narrow canal and this is wide. Sapperton was designed to be 15ft wide and 15ft high at the crown, with a horseshoe shaped profile. In all, twenty-five shafts were sunk, and when work was completed in 1789 it was said to have been so accurately driven that a spectator standing at one portal could see daylight at the far end. Such accuracy would have seemed to bode well for the future: appearances were deceptive.

*The Coates end of Sapperton tunnel, approached down a deep cutting. Restoration has brought out the superb classical features of the portico, carved out of local Cotswold stone.*

Such a great work needed to be recognized architecturally. At the Daneway end, where one of the company's conventional cottages was built, the style was Gothic with pinnacles and battlements. The far end at Coates was even grander. Here the style is classical, the portals flanked by pillars, roundels and round-headed niches. It was said that the intention had been to fill the latter with statues, one of Father Thames, the other Sabrina, goddess of the Severn. It seems they never arrived, and the inscription intended for the scroll above the portal was never carved. The approach to the Coates end is along a deep cutting, above which the company built a lodging house for the tunnellers. It was originally a three-storey, bow-fronted building, with a dormitory running the length of the top storey. As at Daneway, Tunnel House became a pub after construction was over, but lost its upper storey in a fire.

Although the centre section of the tunnel has now collapsed, it is possible to explore some way in by boat from the Coates entrance. Life would have been simple for tunnellers if hills were conveniently uniform in structure, but they seldom are. In this case, beneath the soil there were two varieties of oolitic limestone and deposits of Fuller's Earth, the latter a greyish green rock, rather like a solidified clay and very unstable. The sections through Fuller's Earth and in places where the oolite was of poor quality had to be lined, generally with three layers of brick. To keep the floor of the tunnel watertight it was lined with puddled clay, and in the unlined sections this had to be kept in place by low retaining walls. The section nearest the mouth is lined with brick and the clear water gives a good view of the pale clay at the bottom. Then one enters an area where the great oolite is exposed, often appearing as immense flat slabs of rock in the roof, while the sides show the remains of the holes drilled for blasting.

Beyond the Coates cutting is a lonely three-storey round house. The extra level was not intended to provide more comfort for the family, as the ground floor was used as a stable. Just beyond the cottage, the GWR line between Stroud and Swindon crosses the canal on a high, skew bridge. The next object facing the engineers was a knobbly hill, crowned by an Iron Age fort. This is now the summit level of the canal, so the canal was kept on its contour, clinging to the hillside on a high level above Thames Head, the source of the Thames. With water supply an ever-present problem, the canal company decided to tap the numerous springs of the area. The first attempt used a wind powered pump which proved inadequate, and in 1791 work started on building a house for a Boulton & Watt steam engine which was to pump water up from a 64ft deep oval well. Engines came and went, the last on the site being installed in 1912. Little can now be seen at this somewhat inaccessible site. Indeed, little remains of any canal structures on this long abandoned eastern end. A massive embankment, with a stone revetment, leads up to the western side of the main road between Cirencester and Kemble, but all traces of the aqueduct that once crossed the road have gone.

Siddington was an important spot on the eastern section, where the Cirencester arm turned off to the north, and the remains of the locks that began the descent to the Thames can still be seen. The agent's house still stands, but all the buildings of the maintenance yard have been demolished. Access to much of the rest of the canal is difficult, but there is one last site that can be visited. At Inglesham, the last of the round houses can be seen by the site of the river lock that gave access to the Thames. Leaving the Severn for the Trent brings a dead end canal that never did get extended, but remained as built from Chesterfield to the river. There seems no obvious reason why a market town should have needed a canal, especially one that had to make its way through difficult country, with all the expense that entailed. In fact, Chesterfield itself was not the true attraction at all: that was found in the nearby coalfield. Figures for 1789, thirteen years after the canal was opened, shows coal representing well over half of all the cargo weight carried and, more importantly, it brought in two thirds of the total revenue. The importance of

*The Thames at Inglesham. The entrance to the Thames & Severn is overlooked by its round house.*

bringing the canal round by the collieries explains, at least in part, the seemingly arbitrary route the canal follows on its journey between the river and Chesterfield. However, a close look at the line of the canal on an Ordnance Survey map shows very clearly that this was the work of James Brindley, performing his familiar act of hopping from river valley to river valley and contour cutting in between.

The first part of the journey from West Stockwith on the tidal Trent begins near the mouth of the River Idle, which runs through a broad flood plain, criss-crossed with drainage ditches. The canal keeps close to the southern edge of this wetland, and for the first few miles never climbs higher than the ten-metre contour. As one would expect, when the Idle turns the canal turns with it. There is just one interruption to this leisurely progress. The canal which had been a close neighbour to the river at the start has been steadily moving away, hugging the edge of the rising ground on its way east. But the Idle has its source in the south and in turning with it, Brindley was confronted by a ridge running down from Gringley on the Hill. He took a right-angled turn to meet the hill head on, which was pierced by a 154-yard tunnel, driven through solid rock and largely unlined. Once through, the canal heads right back on itself to the west, keeping to the contour before finally completing the manoeuvre to follow the eastern rim of the Idle valley. With many squiggles and squirms the river is followed into Retford.

Up to here, the going had been easy, if not exactly straightforward, and Brindley was quite happy to build a canal that would take keels from the Trent, with locks 15ft wide. The first lock giving access to the river leads into a wide basin, after which there is a modest stagger of five locks up to the outskirts of the town. The locks themselves are basically the same as the familiar narrow locks of other

*The Chesterfield Canal, leaving the River Trent at West Stockwith. This part of the canal was built with broad locks to allow keels from the river to use the waterway.*

*Gringley lock with a traditional lock cottage. The canal takes the easy route up ahead, keeping to the foot of the low ridge of hills for the next mile and a half.*

Brindley canals. At the charmingly named Whitsunday Pie lock, there is the usual brick bridge across the tail, with a broad semi-circular arch. At Retford, however, things begin to change. The Idle is still running on a north-south line, but Brindley was still a long way east of Chesterfield. It became time to swing across to the next valley, to join the River Ryton at Worksop. Up ahead, the country was considerably less congenial for a canal engineer, and Brindley did what he had done elsewhere, abandoned broad locks and turned to narrow. Just how difficult life was to be for the engineer can be seen from the map, with its closely packed contours, and from the lists of engineering features. From the Trent up to Retford lock, including the river lock, there had been just six locks in fifteen miles; there were to be fifty-one locks in the remaining thirty miles. If this was not enough to convince Mr Brindley to go for the narrow option, there were plans for a tunnel at Norwood, exactly matching that at Harecastle, 2,880 yards long. The summit level is 335ft above the mean level of the Trent, and there is a switchback route from there to Chesterfield. When Brindley died in 1772, the work was continued by his brother-in-law Hugh Henshall. However, the most imposing flight, the fifteen-lock Thorpe locks which include two and three-rise staircases are Brindley's work, and prove that he could be daring when the need arose.

The canal prospered for a long time, but eventually came into railway ownership, and by the end of the nineteenth century, the Chesterfield had been allowed to deteriorate, especially at the western end. Norwood tunnel was a

*Retford marks a turning point in the Chesterfield canal, with broad locks giving way to narrow. There are still reminders of commercial activity in the town, as in this small converted building with its former loading bays.*

constant source of problems. Its location in the heart of a coal mining area made it particularly prone to subsidence, and roof falls were all too common. In 1907 the company decided enough was enough, and no more repairs were carried out. A twenty-mile section of the line was simply abandoned, from the colliery wharf on the outskirts of Worksop all the way back to Chesterfield. There was still traffic on the eastern end, with grain boats working between Worksop and the Trent, though in ever decreasing numbers. Happily, there was just enough movement to keep that part of the canal open, and in 1969 the twenty-six mile stretch was designated as a cruiseway and its condition was gradually improved. The rest was simply abandoned, but not forgotten. There was water in the five-mile section above Worksop, which was unnavigable but acted as a feeder from the reservoirs at Harthill, near the Norwood tunnel. The prospect of restoring the through link to Chesterfield, with so many locks and so much of the canal buried under later developments, is daunting, but already a great deal has been achieved. A survey of the canal west of Worksop shows not only what has been achieved, but just how much there is of interest remaining along the way.

One of the great centres of activity on the narrow canal was Worksop. Approaching the town from the east, one first encounters the canal-orientated buildings that looked east to the rich, agricultural land for their raw materials. The first prominent group near the town centre contains an old brewery, its buildings aligned through a series of shallow angles to follow the gently curving lines of the waterway. Begun as the Prior Well Brewery, enlarging to become the Worksop and Retford Brewery, it now houses offices. Just across the road from the main brewery entrance is what seems from the canal to be a conventional row of cottages. Seen from the road, however, it becomes clear that the houses have been created by dividing up an old, stone built warehouse. Continuing on past a large Victorian grain mill, modernized but still in use, one arrives at what is historically one of the most important set of buildings on the canal. Pickford's began to expand their canal fleet at a great pace throughout the 1790s, while still developing their road haulage business. At Worksop, the two came together. The former Pickford's warehouse is a brick building with the familiar array of loading bays and a regular pattern of windows, each topped by a segmented arch, the whole structure covered by a hipped, slate roof. What is different is the two-storey extension built over an arch straddling the canal. It is a very striking feature, with prominent stone voussoirs to the arch, and walking the towpath under the arch you can look up to see the timber beams supporting the warehouse floor and a square trapdoor for loading and unloading from boats moored underneath. Beside the warehouse is a wharf with an old hand crane and behind it a yard with stabling. The town approach was through a gateway of brick pillars, capped in stone, with movement controlled from the adjoining office. Pickford's abandoned canal carrying in 1847 in the face of railway competition and concentrated on their original trade, carrying goods by road. Recent renovations have seen the office converted into a pub and, at the time of writing, the warehouse was going through the latest of a series of transformations.

Leaving Worksop, everything begins to change as the unmistakably artificial hills of colliery spoil heaps rise up above the canal, but these are now just lonely reminders of an age that has otherwise been erased from the landscape. At Rhodesia, canal rebuilding has deliberately echoed the style of old, with a very humpy hump-backed bridge over the tail of the lock. Built out of reused bricks it has a patina of age, even though it was only completed in 1999. Further along are the three Shireoaks locks. The bye weir of the bottom lock falls down as a miniature cascade, providing a built-in water feature for the house alongside. Above the top lock, the site of Shireoaks Colliery is now a marina, and it is an indication of just how great the transformation has been that when the author visited the site early in 2001, he spotted a kingfisher flitting over a stretch of water where not so long ago coal was being loaded on dry land at the pithead. There is one lasting reminder of mining activity in the area: subsidence. As a result a new low-rise lock had to be built by the restorers to cope with the changes in land levels from the days when Brindley first visited the area on his slow, plodding mare.

The route continues on to the canalside village of Turnerwood. The houses lined up along the wharf are contemporary with the canal, some still retaining their original, small-paned casement windows. Here, lock restoration has seen the first of the two-rise staircases brought back into use. All the time, the ground is getting more hilly and Brindley was forced to go against his natural instincts and make deep cuttings through the rising ground. At the approach to Kiveton Park,

*The scene may look traditional but road realignment has caused a certain amount of rebuilding on the Chesterfield. The little hump-backed bridge at Haggonfield lock, Rhodesia, was only completed in 1999.*

*The most daunting task facing the restorers of the Chesterfield Canal is repair of the many locks, which include three-lock staircases on the Norwood and Thorpe flights. The illustration shows one of the latter, with its three empty chambers.*

the cutting has been made even more dramatic with the arrival of the railway. A high, retaining wall of rough, stone blocks lines the approach to the station. Above this wall were sidings, and there are still indications of trans-shipment devices between the two levels. At the station itself, the canal is crossed by a high road bridge with a yard and wharf nearby.

Beyond Kiveton Park, the canal disappears into the now derelict Norwood tunnel, and when it emerges on the far side the restoration work becomes more patchy with some areas derelict and inaccessible. Where it is in water, there are some intriguing contrasts to be seen. At Hollingwood there is a restored lock, and an odd, quite tiny and very narrow cottage, linking road and canal, but now in a very sorry state, boarded up and forlorn. Here the canal sits at the centre of a network of old colliery lines and sidings, now unused, their bridges dismantled. Of all the canals looked at so far, this is perhaps the most dramatic example of a scene where the railways that killed the canal trade have themselves died, while the canal has been reborn. At the Chesterfield end, there is another curious contrast. Canal and towpath have been incorporated into a linear country park, with a visitor centre by Tapton lock, but the name 'Lock Keeper' does not live on – it has been appropriated by a modern hotel on the far side of the main road. The canal park continues on a little further heading towards the centre of Chesterfield itself, with its famous crooked spire.

*A happier sight than the scene at Thorpe. Here Dixon's lock, near Chesterfield, is fully restored together with its neat, hump-backed brick bridge over the tail.*

Chesterfield may not have been an obvious candidate for a canal, but eighteenth century Chester was almost desperate for one. There was a time when Chester had been the premier port in north-west England, but as early as 1677 the writer Andrew Yarranton was noting that trade was 'much decayed' and 'that old great City in danger of being ruin'd'. The city fathers had been reluctant to raid the coffers for funds to keep the Dee dredged, let alone for making improvements, and as a result Liverpool and the Mersey were taking trade away from Chester and the Dee. The passing of the Trent & Mersey Act seemed likely to make matters worse, giving Liverpool new connections with the interior. Very late in the day, the merchants of Chester decided something had to be done and they proposed building a canal from the Dee at Chester to the Trent & Mersey at Middlewich, with a short branch down to the prosperous salt town of Nantwich. Nothing went right. The Trent & Mersey had no intention of seeing any trade diverting to the Dee, and when the Chester Act was passed in 1772 there was a specific proviso that there should *not* be a connection at Middlewich. As that had been the main reason for building the canal in the first place there seemed little point in continuing, but work went ahead anyway as a direct line to Nantwich. There were even more complications, with arguments over how the Dee connection should be made and as a result this canal, a mere nineteen miles long and following an easy route across the Cheshire plain, was not opened until 1779 and, not surprisingly, was a financial disaster. It was rescued from oblivion in 1796 when the act was passed for the construction of the Ellesmere Canal, now better known as the Llangollen Canal, which joined the Chester canal and also extended northward to the Mersey where a new canal town and docks were built, and named Ellesmere Port. There were to be further connections. The long hoped-for link to Middlewich was finally made, fifty-four years after it was first proposed, and a new line was built south from Nantwich, the Birmingham & Liverpool Junction Canal. A great deal of activity now surrounded the Chester Canal, but nothing could restore the fortunes of the port of Chester. The changes did, however, profoundly affect the features on the original canal, as successive owners made changes and improvements.

Few canals presented such an easy task to the engineers as this, though the dithering Chester proprietors called in a hatful of engineers to make reports to make sure they had the right answers. The route seems remarkably direct for an early canal, but merely reflects the flat, easy nature of the ground to be covered. It was built, like other canals linked to river navigations, as a barge canal with locks 74ft by 14ft 6in. The greatest challenge was presented by Chester itself. The city has its origins with the Romans, when the sandstone outcrop standing high above the Dee was an obvious site for a fort, under whose protection the city grew. It still retains the basic Roman street pattern, but the centre is enclosed by high medieval walls. The canal was never going to go through the city, so it had to skirt the northern wall and force a way through the rock at the base.

The Chester end of the canal is one of those areas where much has changed. With the construction of the line to Ellesmere Port, the original drop down to the Dee was lost and a new branch constructed. Old and new canal meet at Tower Wharf, which became an important point on the Shropshire Union Canal system, established after the completion of the Birmingham & Liverpool Junction Canal in 1835. Thomas Telford was Chief Engineer for the new canal, and he made many changes to the older links. A grand square warehouse, with hipped roof and loading bays has walls falling sheer to the water. It was extended at a later date by a structure in quite a different style, built over arches creating shipping holes and treated with a certain stylishness, its tall, round-headed windows separated by pilasters. The original Chester Canal Co. had no money for such fripperies. Further along the canal, a variety of other buildings are met which also date from the later improvements. In Chester itself, a lock cottage with relieving arches round the windows is built to the pattern Telford had first used on the Ellesmere Canal. Among the elegant features met along the way are the lock lobbies, rest places and stores for lengthmen. These are circular structures, neatly fitted with curved wooden doors, with a stone parapet and domed roof sprouting a central chimney.

From Tower Wharf the canal climbs steeply up through the three inter-connected locks of the Northgate Staircase. Cut out of the solid rock, they lift the canal 33ft from the basin. Originally, a further two locks led straight down to the Dee. Now the canal begins its spectacular progress round the city walls, closed into its rocky cutting, before emerging out into the suburbs. Once clear of the city, the canal takes a direct line through a rural landscape where, instead of industrial buildings lining the route, one finds grain mills scattered along the way. Most of the features are familiar from other canals, though there are always special points

*Looking remarkably like a moat round a castle, the Chester Canal skirts the medieval walls of the city.*

to look out for, such as the recesses built into bridge abutments to hold stop planks. There was also a unique solution to a difficult problem. There were two conventional locks at Beeston, but one of them, built in sand, suffered numerous collapses. When the Chester became a vital link in the expanding system, Thomas Telford decided to look for a permanent solution to the problem. He created what was, in effect, a giant open-topped box of angled iron plates which was set in the lock pit to replace the masonry, creating the unique Beeston Iron Lock.

The formation of the Shropshire Union, an amalgam of several canals including the Chester, in the nineteenth century added more new buildings. These included a new stable block beside the two-lock staircase at Bunbury. This was already a busy spot with wharf, warehouse and lock cottage, but the stables stand out for their trim design, with round-headed windows and doors and ventilation cowls in the roof. Canal horses were not pampered beasts and most canal companies were content to let boatmen make their own arrangements for stabling and fodder, but the Shropshire Union was unusual in running its own fleet, which by the end of the nineteenth century had grown to over four hundred narrow boats. The stables were an investment, and there was even a vet on duty.

Beyond Bunbury, the long awaited Middlewich branch leads away under a typical long, low junction bridge, soon followed by the next meeting point of Hurleston Junction and the start of the Llangollen line. There is only a little way

*Looking down on the canal from Northgate Bridge in Chester one can see how the engineers had to carve a cutting through the sandstone on which the city is built.*

to go now before the old Chester Canal ended at Nantwich Basin. It is somehow typical of the Chester that it never really reached the town at all, coming to a halt about a mile from the centre. The basin lies just off the present main line, which now makes an end-to-end junction with Telford's canal from Birmingham.

The Chester Canal would have been a complete failure, but for later developments. The next in this ragbag of canals was even shorter, and although it too was to become part of a more extended system, it thrived perfectly well on its own. The Huddersfield Broad Canal was built with a specific end in mind, and was, like the Bridgewater, privately promoted by a young man. Sir John Ramsden was so young, in fact, that he was still a minor when the scheme was begun, and had to leave the official side of parliamentary promotion to his mother and uncle. The Ramsden family owned most of Huddersfield in the mid-eighteenth century, and were enthusiastic promoters of the town's industrial development – and that included canal building. Proposals were first put forward in 1768, but as a result of opposition from the local turnpike road trusts, the act was not approved until 1774. Work began on the canal that was to link Huddersfield to the Calder & Hebble Navigation at Cooper Bridge, $3\frac{1}{2}$ miles away. It was built to take Yorkshire keels, with locks 58ft by 14ft 3ins. There were nine of these in all and the canal was opened in 1776. It may seem a long time for the completion of such a short canal, but as it was privately funded, the owners were more cautious than companies that could call on a large body of shareholders for extra funds. There is also rather more to it than is immediately obvious, for the top mile and a half was dug very deep to create a reservoir. This was only partly a practical measure: it was also a sop to local mill owners who feared that water would be drawn away from their factories.

The line of the canal follows the River Colne, which flows down from the Pennines to reach the Calder close to the canal junction at Cooper Bridge. Much has changed on this canal since it was first opened. The lock cottage by lock one looks unusually grand, but closer inspection shows that it is in fact two cottages now joined together. The line that was constructed through open country has now been largely engulfed by the spread of Huddersfield – an expansion which it helped to create. Railways and their long, high viaducts are a dominant feature, and road bridges have been widened to cope with modern traffic. Lock three does have its original bridge in place, and one can see that cost saving was more important than convenience. As on the Droitwich canal, the bridge over the tail of the lock is so close to the bottom gates that stumpy, cranked balance beams have to be used.

There is one extraordinary structure near the town centre, Locomotive Bridge. This is not, as its name might suggest, a railway bridge, but a lift bridge. An iron gantry has pulleys at its four corners, carrying two chains, one end attached to the platform, while counterweights are suspended at the other, the whole contraption operated by a hand wheel. It was built in 1865, apparently replacing a conventional swing bridge. Clearly it would have been impossible to lift a wide bridge over a broad canal using no more leverage than the usual balance beam, but even so it looks remarkably like the sort of thing youngsters used to build in the days of the Meccano set.

The canal now ends at Apsley basin where the more interesting buildings disappeared in a road-widening scheme of the 1960s. Here the Broad Canal meets the Huddersfield Narrow Canal, first opened throughout in 1811 and reopened after a major restoration effort in 2001. The basin was once an important interchange, for the Yorkshire keels were too wide for the narrow canal and the narrow boats too long for the broad. Now it is a marina.

The Erewash Canal was, like the Chesterfield, primarily seen as a way to improve the carriage of coal from the pits to the Trent. It terminates at Langley Mill, close by D.H. Lawrence's birthplace of Eastwood and deep in the heart of the mining country he described in novels and stories. The area is still dominated by spoil heaps and flashes. It was the first canal to penetrate this region, though it was soon to be followed by others poking their watery fingers towards yet more mines and factories. Begun in 1777, it was completed under the direction of John Varley within two years. It so closely follows the line of the River Erewash throughout its length that it can almost be considered a river navigation rather than an artificial canal. There are fourteen locks, all 14ft 3in wide, but reducing in length from 78ft to 72ft above Tamworth Road Bridge. Unlike the Huddersfield situation, there was never going to be a problem with trans-shipment between barges and narrow boats. The canal was just the kind of enterprise that was bound to succeed in its day. It met the Duke of Bridgewater's famous dictum that the successful canal should have 'coal at the heel of it'. Along its banks are to be seen works that vary from foundries that produced massive iron castings to factories built to turn out delicate lace. It is also clear why traffic would ultimately dwindle and die, for the later railways can be seen snaking all over the Erewash valley – main lines, branch lines, colliery lines and lines to industrial sidings. In this instance, however, the Erewash owners helped to speed their own demise. Having made a great deal of money when they had a monopoly of the coal trade, they declined to reduce prices when competition threatened, leaving the disgruntled colliery owners as eager railway promoters.

The beginning at the junction with the Trent sees a complex of transport routes all coming together. The Trent itself has divided upstream of this point, the river flowing down over Thrumpton Weir, while the navigation channel goes down through Cranfleet Lock. Here, where natural river and cutting are reunited, the Erewash turns away to the north, while the Soar Navigation heads off south to Leicester. Railways, too, head off to all points of the compass, viaducts meeting in a triangular junction above the waterways. The canal turns off under a footbridge, carrying the towpath of the Trent Navigation, and at once emerges in a holding basin below the first lock. This has stepped sides, which are very popular with people who like to sit around and watch the movement of the boats, but they have a very practical purpose. River levels can change very dramatically, and as the level in this basin is always the same as that on the river, boats will lie alongside the steps, no matter what the height of the water. It is a spot well endowed with pubs, even if there have been considerable changes. The Trent Navigation Inn looks out over the river, but in 1791, the canal company built their own pub beside the lock, which has gone through a number of changes and has ended up as tea rooms, its

*The start of the Erewash Canal at Trent Lock, overlooked by the former canal pub. The stepped basin allows for changes in river levels. Here the river is high and flood water has swept debris into the canal.*

place usurped by the grander and more recent Steamboat Inn. The older building, however, still preserves its original eighteenth century character, with a strictly symmetrical frontage, two large windows flanking the central door, and three windows on the first floor, the central opening being narrower than the other two to preserve the regularity.

Once out of the lock, the canal has yet another encounter with the rivals, as three railway bridges cross the line in quick succession. But there was scope for co-operation. In among the bridges is the entrance to Sheetstores Basin, the odd name deriving from the days when tarpaulin sheets were made here. More importantly, it was here that coal was exchanged between boats and railway wagons.

The canal continues through Long Eaton and Sandiacre, in the heart of the lace making industry. All the developments post-date the canal, as the first lace-making machine did not appear until 1809, when John Heathcoat invented his plain-net machine. The mills by the canal belong very much to the steam age and as if inspired by the delicacy of the end product, boast ornate decoration in their tall chimneys. There is a particularly fine example at Sandiacre, where the lock has one of the few surviving original lock cottages. At this point, the Erewash is joined by the now derelict Derby Canal, begun in 1793. Beyond the bridge carrying the M1, lace making gives way to iron making and the Stanton iron works. The Nutbrook Canal, another 1793 venture, turned off here and ran right through the works. Just

$4\frac{1}{2}$ miles long, it barely survived to celebrate its centenary, abandoned in 1895. The Erewash is crossed by the railway bridge, carrying the branch line that took away the canal trade. A third derelict canal can now be seen, following the line of the Erewash, but on the opposite bank and at a higher level. This is the Nottingham Canal which, like the other two, came into railway ownership and withered on the vine. The Erewash survived longer only because it managed to maintain its independence. Shipley Gate, with its lock-side stables, continued to serve as an interchange wharf even after traffic had died on the surrounding canals. Here, the canal finally crosses the Erewash on a small aqueduct, which is not very imposing but has an unusual history. The natural crossing point to keep engineering works to a minimum was here, close to the lock, but the river was in the wrong place. So, the aqueduct was built over dry land, a watercourse cut underneath it and the Erewash diverted into the new channel. The canal ends at the Great Northern Basin, which actually marked the end of the Nottingham Canal. It also marks the beginning of the Cromford Canal, our last canal from the 1780s.

The Cromford was built as an extension of the Erewash, heading off towards the Derbyshire town where Sir Richard Arkwright had built his pioneering water-powered cotton mill in 1771. Construction began in 1789 under William Jessop, who had learned his profession under the great engineer John Smeaton. It was to be his first major canal, but by no means his last. The task he faced

*Stone distance posts rarely survive on the canals but this roughly carved example on the Erewash is an exception.*

*The immense chimney of a nineteenth-century lace mill soars above the Erewash Canal at Sandiacre.*

was far greater than that presented by leading a canal up a river valley. As he himself wrote, 'In a District of Country, such as this is proposed to pass through, rugged and Mountainous, it will at first sight strike an observer, as very ineligible for such a project.' One can see why he was dismayed. The whole route was just $14\frac{1}{2}$ miles long, with a 2 mile branch, but in that distance there were to be four tunnels, three of them short, but the fourth, Butterley Tunnel, was 2,966 yards long. To add to the engineering headaches, there were to be two big aqueducts, across the Amber and the Derwent. Three reservoirs also had to be constructed, the largest at Butterley covering fifty acres. Jessop decided to build the canal to two gauges, a broad canal with wide locks from Langley Mill to the eastern end of Butterley tunnel, but the tunnel itself was only to be nine feet wide and the remainder of the canal into Cromford would remain narrow. Even though he had tried to minimize the difficulties, Jessop had trouble with both aqueducts. Part of the Amber aqueduct, 200 yards long and 50ft high collapsed, and Jessop bravely took the blame on himself and paid for the repairs. Then in 1793, a crack appeared in the Derwent aqueduct. Jessop had tried to economize in the use of material to keep within the approved budget, but had gone too far. The walls proved to be not thick enough and had to be reinforced and the cracks were closed with iron tie bars.

*The Leawood aqueduct carrying the Cromford Canal over the River Derwent, with the tall chimney of the pumping station, that supplied the canal with water from the river, poking above the trees.* (A. Burton).

The Butterley tunnel, which might have been thought of as the greater problem, proved remarkably trouble free during construction. Thirty-three shafts were sunk, and the tunnel was built with an unusual cross section, 9ft wide but only 8ft high at the crown, with a very flattened invert arch at the bottom. It was mostly brick-lined and had no towpath. It has not survived, but this time through no fault of Jessop's. It was literally undermined by a nearby colliery and collapsed. It was not considered worth reopening and the whole canal was closed in 1944. Very little of the canal has survived between Langley Mill and Ambergate, though the Butterley Reservoir is still in water and is very impressive, with a massive retaining embankment, 33ft high and 12ft wide at the top. Happily there is a lot to see on the remaining section to Cromford.

The canal remains on the level once it has emerged from Butterley tunnel, but the going was still far from easy. Only a mile-and-a-half along the way, it plunged underground again in the ninety-six yard Bullbridge tunnel, which unlike Butterley was built with a towpath. From here the canal swings north up the narrow Derwent valley, with hills rising steeply on either side. All the major transport routes – road, rail and canal – are squeezed together. At Leawood, the railway engineers opted for a tunnel through a spur of the hills that cut across their route, but Jessop had taken the other option of crossing the Derwent to find an easier passage on the west bank.

The aqueduct may have caused him trouble and expense, but it is a majestic structure, 600ft long and 30ft high, crossing the river in a single 80ft span arch. It was built of locally quarried gritstone, with a neatly rounded top to the parapets.

At the far end is the Leawood pumping station, housing a steam engine that was used to pump water from the Derwent into the canal. The narrow engine house presents a sophisticated front to the world. Built of rusticated gritstone blocks, it has dressed stone at the quoins and around the round-headed window; the door is flanked by pilasters, and the whole is topped by a prominent pediment. The tall stack has an unusually wide parapet, perhaps to prevent any possible nuisance from down draughts in this narrow valley. Alongside is the boiler house with two double doors in front of the two boilers. The present preserved engine is a typical beam engine with a sixty-inch cylinder, which was capable of delivering 2,000 gallons of water a minute into the canal. At the south end of the aqueduct is the start of a short branch, now derelict, to Lea Mills. A dilapidated lock cottage stands near this important section of canal. Built of local stone with a stone slate roof, it is rather crudely built with roughly cut stone surrounds to windows and doors.

From the aqueduct the canal continued comparatively uneventfully to Cromford, ending at a wharf and small warehouse. Here water was supplied from Cromford Sough, a drainage channel built to de-water the nearby Dove Gang lead mine. This same water supply was also used to turn the wheels of Arkwright's mill, which can still be seen just across the road. This is really the end of the Cromford story as far as early developments are concerned, but it is worth pointing out that even when a canal was completed and open for business, this did not mean that all development came to an end. In 1814, plans were put forward for a tramway that would cross the hills of the Peak District to link up with the Peak Forest Canal at Whaley Bridge. It was not very long, just thirty-three miles, but it had a summit 990ft above the level of the Cromford Canal, so that it certainly earned the 'high' part of its name, The Cromford & High Peak Railway. Traffic was to be partly horse drawn, but the hills were conquered by inclines, up and down which trucks were cable hauled by a steam winding engine set at the top. The engineer was Josias Jessop, William's son. The line began at the transit shed on the canal wharf at High Peak Junction. The main building is in two parts: a substantial awning, supported by cast iron columns, covering the boats and the open wharf, and a solid stone building with wide doors at the Cromford end, through which the tramway waggons could be trundled. In later years, the level parts of the line used steam locomotives, serviced in the nearby maintenance buildings, now preserved. Here one can still see the original fish-bellied rails mounted on stone sleeper blocks.

This book has dealt with canals begun before 1790, with what were often modest ambitions. With the Cromford Canal we can see that this is only a part of a continuous process. William Jessop learned some hard lessons in building the Cromford, but went on to become the most successful canal engineer of the 1790s, the years of canal mania, and here we can see his son taking the story on into the dawn of the railway age. Things had indeed come a long way since the days when the Duke of Bridgewater decided he needed a better way to get his coal to Manchester.

# Gazetteer

The following list gives the more interesting sites to be found on the canals covered in this book. The standard Ordnance Survey system of grid references is used with one small variation. The first numbers quoted give the number of the Landranger (1:50,000) map on which the feature appears. This is followed by either a 4 or 6 figure number. The former gives a reference to features such as flights of locks and basins that spread over a large area; the latter give a more exact location for specific features, such as bridges and warehouses.

## Chapter 1

| | | |
|---|---|---|
| Car Dyke: | The clearest section can be seen beside the A1 | 0154/4866 |
| River Avon: | The flash lock remains are by Jubilee Bridge | 150/000456 |
| | Exeter Ship Canal: Turf lock | 192/964860 |
| | Custom House Quay | 192/9292 |
| River Wye: | Site of Tintern boat yard | 162/533003 |
| | Redbrook wharf | 162/5309 |
| River Lugg: | Mordiford bridge and flash lock | 149/569376 |
| Kennet Navigation: | Monkey Marsh lock | 174/525663 |
| | Aldermaston lock | 175/601672 |

## Chapter 2

| | | |
|---|---|---|
| Bridgewater Canal: | Worsley Delph | 109/7400 |
| | Barton aqueduct | 109/767976 |
| | Bollin bank and aqueduct | 109/7287 |
| | The Duke's Dock, Liverpool | 108/3489 |

## Chapter 3

| | | |
|---|---|---|
| Trent & Mersey Canal: | Shardlow | 129/4430 |
| | Harecastle tunnel, northern end | 118/8354 |
| | Armitage 'tunnel' | 128/0716 |
| | Etruscan bone and flint mill | 118/872468 |
| | Barnton tunnel | 118/7463 |
| | Saltersford tunnel | 118/6275 |
| | Preston Brook | 108/5680 |
| Caldon Canal: | Cheddleton flint mill | 118/973525 |
| | Hazelhurst aqueduct | 118/954536 |
| | Froghall wharf | 119/0247 |
| | Rudyard Lake | 118/9459 |

## Chapter 4

| | | |
|---|---|---|
| Staffs & Worcester: | Haywood junction and Trent aqueduct | 127/9922 |
| | Sow aqueduct | 127/973215 |
| | Gailey wharf | 127/920105 |
| | Cookley tunnel and Debdale lock | 138/8480 |
| | The Bratch | 139/865933 |
| | Stourport basins | 138/8171 |
| Oxford Canal: | Canal offices, Bulwarks Lane | 164/5106 |
| | Thrupp | 164/4815 |
| | Shipton Weir lock | 164/487170 |
| | Fenny Compton 'tunnel' | 151/4352 |
| | Wormleighton hill | 151/4355 |
| | Napton locks (bottom) | 151/4560 |
| | Newbold on Avon tunnel | 140/486772 |
| | Brinklow 'aqueduct' | 140/4480 |
| | Hawkesbury junction | 140/3684 |
| Coventry Canal: | Coventry basin | 140/333796 |
| | Atherstone locks | 140/3097 |
| | Hartshill yard | 140/328952 |

## Chapter 5

| | | |
|---|---|---|
| Birmingham Canal: | Cambrian wharf | 139/059868 |
| | Rotton Park reservoir | 139/0486 |
| | Stewart aqueduct, Spon Lane | 139/003897 |
| | Wolverhampton locks (top) | 139/9099 |
| Dudley Canal: | Dudley tunnel and Black Country Museum | 139/9491 |
| | Delph locks | 139/8986 |
| Stourbridge Canal: | Stourbridge locks (bottom) | 139/8986 |
| B'ham & Fazeley Canal: | Salford junction (Spaghetti Junction) | 139/0990 |

## Chapter 6

| | | |
|---|---|---|
| Leeds & L'pool Canal: | Leeds office | 104/296330 |
| | Junction with Bradford Canal, Shipley | 104/152377 |
| | First Aire aqueduct | 104/132382 |
| | Bingley Five Rise | 104/1039 |
| | Springs Branch, Skipton | 103/9952 |
| | Second Aire aqueduct | 103/9153 |
| | Greenberfield locks | 103/8848 |
| | Foulridge tunnel | 103/8842 |

|  |  |  |
|---|---|---|
|  | Burnley mile | 103/8432 |
|  | Johnson's Hillock junction | 102/5920 |
|  | Wigan Pier | 108/577053 |
|  | Stanley Dock, Liverpool | 108/338922 |

## Chapter 7

|  |  |  |
|---|---|---|
| Droitwich Canal: | Ladywood lock | 150/868611 |
| Stroudwater Canal: | Ryeford double lock | 162/819047 |
|  | Wallbridge company office | 162/847050 |
| Thames & Severn Canal: | Chalford wharf | 163/892025 |
|  | Sapperton tunnel, Daneway | 163/9403 |
|  | Sapperton tunnel, Coates | 163/9600 |
|  | Inglesham round house | 163/204988 |
| Chesterfield Canal: | West Stockwith basin | 112/7894 |
|  | Drakeholes tunnel | 112/7090 |
|  | Whitsunday Pie lock | 120/721820 |
|  | Pickford's warehouse, Worksop | 120/585793 |
|  | Turnerwood village and locks | 120/5481 |
|  | Tapton visitor centre, Chesterfield | 119/387731 |
| Chester Canal: | Tower Wharf | 117/3966 |
|  | Beeston iron lock | 117/553599 |
|  | Bunbury locks | 117/5759 |
|  | Nantwich basin | 118/6352 |
| Huddersfield Broad Canal: | Locomotive bridge | 110/149168 |
| Erewash Canal: | Trent Lock | 129/4931 |
|  | Sandiacre lock | 129/482358 |
|  | Great Northern basin | 129/4547 |
| Cromford Canal: | Leawood aqueduct | 119/3155 |
|  | Cromford & High Peak Railway wharf | 119/314557 |
|  | Cromford wharf | 119/3056 |

# Index